A Word
From Lou

A WORD FROM LOU

Commentary, Observations, and Advice for
Law Students, Young Lawyers, Old Lawyers,
and Folks Who Like Reading Such Stuff

By Lou Scofield

STORYARTSMEDIA

Published by Story Arts Media
Sonoma, California
www.storyartsmedia.com

ISBN: 978-0-9970672-6-2
Library of Congress Control Number: 2019911018

Cover and Interior Design: Joseph Daniel

POD Edition
Printed in the United States

This book is dedicated to my children,
each of whom is my treasure:
Christopher Aiken Scofield, Nicholas Dickens Scofield,
and Emma Colleen Scofield.

AUTHOR'S NOTE

This book is a collection of columns originally published in *The Association Press*, a biannual publication of the Association of Defense Trial Attorneys. The ADTA is an organization made up of courtroom lawyers with law practices that involve civil cases, primarily on the defense side.

Membership in the ADTA is quite an honor. Only one Prime Member is allowed per city (or per 1,000,000 in population for large cities). Skill, reputation, and professionalism are the attributes leading to membership, or, in my case, remarkable good looks and charm . . . ahem.

A couple of decades ago I was given instructions to write the column and to "make it about practicing law . . . and sprinkle in some humor if you want." So began these twice-yearly commentary, observation, and advice columns exposing the ADTA membership to the wandering mind (or, I would say, stunning wisdom) of yours truly.

As is inevitable with such a thing, with the passage of time, and accumulation of enough articles, someone said, "Say, why don't you pull them together into a book?" "Why not?" I asked myself. It's a lot easier than writing a real book. So here it is.

- Lou Scofield
Beaumont, Texas
August, 2019

P.S. By the way, any resemblance of anyone or anything in this book to any person, organization, or events, real or fictional, is purely coincidental, even if I name them!

TABLE OF CONTENTS

The author, very fresh out of law school, and just starting his career over 40 years ago.

BY LOU SCOFIELD

Where It All Starts

Spring 2017

There is a town I know where people still pull over in their cars and stop as a funeral procession goes by. Many pedestrians stop as well, and men can be seen taking off their hats in honor of the person who passed and in sympathy for those grieving.

There is a town I know where high-school choirs sing at annual Christmas shows, and whose students take the craft so seriously, and work so well and hard, that they even do justice to the Christmas portion of Handel's Messiah...and, of course, the audience stands during the singing of the "Hallelujah Chorus."

There is a town I know where people of all races and politics join each other worshiping in church, or together enjoy carnivals and community fairs, and compete fiercely at amateur sporting events representing company teams.

There is a town I know where the tough drinking joints are few, and the nice watering holes are many. Many have great food, live music, dancing, and an air of youth and freedom. Some are routinely populated by lawyers, judges, and business leaders discussing business, or assiduously avoiding discussion of business.

There is a town I know where the culture and community is such that almost everybody has a notable degree of self-respect, which makes tolerance of others easy.

There is a town I know where most work is blue-collar, with an aging population of the folks who built literally hundreds of liberty ships to help win the war, burned up their youth opening up the disease-infested oilfields of Venezuela, and have refined the foundation of our modern civilization: oil.

There is a town I know where the population is not too small, so you have your privacy, but is small enough that you always see someone you know when you are out and about. Where people do not take themselves too seriously, and live out their lives in a security provided by the "background music" of decency, honor, and rule of law.

There is a town I know where, yes, there are drug dealers, thieves, assailants, and an occasional killer, and where the unjust suffering of the victims is noticed by everyone, and the tragedy (and swift punishment) of the perpetrators is noticed as well. It is the very atmosphere of the culture, an unspoken understanding that we are all the victims of such evil and disorder, and an unspoken consensus that it will not be tolerated.

There is a town I know where the meager downtown skyline is formed by a half-dozen multi-story office buildings, the tallest of which is seventeen stories. At street level there are a few eating establishments, two libraries, an art museum, a couple of churches, a Catholic basilica, a synagogue, a mosque, a park sculpture of Martin Luther King Jr., and courthouse sculptures of several great lawyers who have passed, most of whom were friends and partners of mine.

When I started practice it was common to walk from our office to the state courthouse to the south, or the federal courthouse to the north (no, you snarky souls, I did not ride horseback to the jail). Most of the local law firms had their offices downtown, and sometimes opposing lawyers in a trial or hearing would run into one another walking along the way. They would pass the time talking of their families and children, then step up the stairs to the arena.

There is a town I know where the courts are, for the most part, there for the litigants and not for their own sake; where the law is generally respected; and lawyers are generally respected. A minor witness to this attribute is the sheepish, almost apologetic, glance and grin that usually precedes or follows the occasional good-natured lawyer joke—the look and grin being the silent statement of the teller that no real offense was meant, and he knows lawyers are key to all of this.

Some Small Cases

Summer/Fall 2013

As I've added gray hair, my docket grows more serious. Now I handle, almost exclusively, cases involving terrible circumstances: fatalities, amputations, one or more testicles injured or lost . . . they each have their stories. But lessons from the "little cases" can be useful to remember. Here are a few tales that are not too tall.

One of the cases I've tried in a small town north of Beaumont, Texas, involved a big fella—let's call him Mr. Harvey—who claimed he was hurt on the job. We claimed he wasn't. Liability was a toss-up, and the injury involved his low back, an alleged "herniated disc," yet there had been no surgery. In view of this we had made a settlement offer that was respectable. But Mr. Harvey wanted to gamble, so he rejected our offer.

The trial went well, and my case was carried by the live testimony of a grizzled old country doctor who had examined Mr. Harvey for me. On cross-examination, when pressed by Mr. Harvey's lawyer in a somewhat sarcastic fashion, the doctor only got stronger. He turned to the jury and told them that when Mr. Harvey left his office he not only did not have a herniated disc, but "was as healthy as any of you jurors."

The case on liability went well too, owing, in large part, to Mr. Harvey's limited interpersonal skills. So you will not be surprised to learn that the jury poured him out.

After the verdict was read, and the jury was thanked and filed out of the courtroom, I shook hands with opposing counsel, conferred briefly with my client's representative, then made the mistake of leaving the courthouse at the same time as Mr. Harvey, his wife, and his mother-in-law. They were not accompanied by their lawyer, and they were pissed—and not just in general; they were angry at me, personally.

Imagine that. A sweet, good-natured soul like me . . .

Anyhow, I first realized their state of mind as I neared my truck. They were standing on the other side of it, and my ears began to register the profanities being sent in my direction from all three of them. I should have said nothing, but for some reason I responded, "I'm sorry you feel that way."

Well, that made the pot boil over. "You sure are sorry—you're a sorry, no-good, #$@! . . . " snarled Mr. Harvey. And at this they began to move menacingly along the opposite side of my truck. Now, back then I was terrifically strong, so I figured I had an even chance against the mother-in-law. The wife, on the other hand, was no lily, and was very likely to best me. Plus, as I mentioned earlier, Mr. Harvey was a big fella with limited interpersonal skills (remember?). Therefore, I wisely kept my truck between them and me until they exhausted their vocabulary, which seemed to exhaust them, and they left. It occurred to me later that Mr. Harvey must have left his gun in his other pants.

I don't leave a courthouse anymore at the same time as disgruntled plaintiffs.

Under Texas rules you can use a deposition for any purpose. In trial, reading a deposition to jurors is common, and skilled oral presentation of deposition testimony is necessary.

I was trying a case here in Beaumont in which I needed to present an important segment of an eyewitness deposition to the jury. I did not, however, want to be accused of taking the testimony out of context, or of hiding the other parts of the story of the witness, so I set out to read the entire deposition (only about thirty-five pages long). Sitting in the witness chair, I crossed one leg over the other to get comfortable and began reading to the jury in my finest monotone, to prevent the bulk of the testimony from having any impact.

When I got to the prime segment, of which I wanted everyone to take note, I changed the inflection in my voice, and lifted my eyes to make eye contact with the jury. Half were asleep and would not have heard, let alone remembered, my dramatic rendition of the testimony to come. Rather than be the cad who awakened them, I turned to the judge for assistance. He too was asleep.

I stopped reading and took in the scene. Fortunately, my silence seemed to awaken everyone. I completed the testimony, and the jury got both the point and some rest.

But I don't use that monotone anymore.

I drive like a saint in Hardin County. It is the price of "justice."

Hardin is a county north of Beaumont. It is rural and heavily forested, with a population made up of folks who have lived there for generations and newcomers who commute to work in Beaumont. One of the latter is a client of mine who runs several businesses down here. One night he, and his wife, got in trouble with the local constabulary by throwing a party that disturbed the peaceful tranquility of the forest.

They were charged with a misdemeanor, but not jailed.

They were technically "innocent," and had been treated somewhat roughly in their home by the deputy sheriff. He was from a family who had lived there for generations and, simply put, did not think much of my "newcomer" clients.

So my folks wanted their day in court. It was a very little case, but big to them.

The law they had violated contained, like all criminal statutes, specific elements that had to be proved . . . and an element was missing from the state's proof. During the trial, I cross-examined the deputy, with all the indignation of any Texan wrongly accused. After some tough exchanges, I drew a bitter confession from him that he was missing the critical proof needed to convict.

The case was summarily dismissed by the court. My clients were delighted.

But I now drive like a saint in Hardin County. If I ever get pulled over, even if I can beat the rap, I doubt I will beat the ride.

Fishermen among you, pay attention. I once defended a product liability case in Orange, Texas (just east of Beaumont), against a company that makes the finest fillet knives in the world. They are made of soft, flexible steel, and are wickedly sharp.

The plaintiff, a man of local importance, had had a banner day fishing. He got home with a half-dozen four-to-five-pound speckled trout. He was on his back porch carving fillets from them when his hand slipped down the handle of his knife, onto the wicked blade. It "cut the dickens" out of his hand (apologies to Dan Aykroyd as Julia Child in the classic SNL skit). Tendons, ligaments, blood—he was cut to the bone. It messed up his day.

So he sued my client. He figured a knife that sharp should have had a guard of some kind.

I defended the case exactly as each of you would

have. We did minimal written discovery, took no depositions, and set it for jury trial. During voir dire I asked the panel to raise their hands, and keep them up, if they had ever cut themselves with a knife. All the hands went up. I then asked how many ever blamed the knife. All hands went down . . . they were conditioned.

On cross-examination of the plaintiff I only had him detail the technique he used to carve up his catch. Yep, in the process he used his "knife hand" to handle the fish, and in doing so covered his hand and the knife handle with slime. As he saw it, though, such was all the more reason a notch or guard of some sort was needed.

Then the plaintiff called out his big gun, an expert witness of unimpeachable credentials: Billy Halfin. Mr. Halfin is a famous local celebrity outdoorsman with a radio show, TV spots, magazine articles, the works. He is liked by all because he is honest, kind, and "country," and knows the outdoors. He testified that this knife should have had a hilt or finger notch on the handle, and that such features could have prevented this accident.

On cross-examination I said that I'd bet he always had a knife in his pocket. He did (this was long before metal detectors in every courthouse). I asked if we could see it. He showed it to us. It was a classic folding pocketknife. No hilt or notch in the handle. I showed it to the jury. Then I asked:

"Mr. Halfin, have you ever cut yourself with a knife?"

"Many times," he replied.

So I followed up, "Did you ever blame the knife?"

He smiled. "Every time!"

The jury loved him . . . but rendered their verdict for my client.

Accessories

Summer 2006

We don't sufficiently acknowledge the importance of accessories to our successful practice of law. For example, I have a "Dictaphone voice processor" on which I dictate my obstructionist pleadings, non-responsive discovery replies, frivolous objections to discovery, motions filled with righteous indignation, intemperate letters to opposing counsel, and pretrial reports to my client and the insurance carrier (predicting disaster unless my considerable courtroom skills carry the day). I don't know how it became a "voice processor" instead of a tape recorder, but I'm not going to question its title because I need it. I recently had a day when it broke down. This event did not reduce me to a useless biomass (as do some mechanical malfunctions), but I was at least partially disabled until they put a replacement on my credenza.

For some of you, the breakdown of a "voice processor" would do little to disrupt your day. But what if I took your smartphone (BlackBerry? Strawberry? Elderberry?) and dropped it into the commode? Eh? What if I did that! What if I put it in your kid's school backpack, so she could use it as a trowel to dig in the playground dirt! Imagine being without these valuable tools. Could you still function? You should be able to. It wasn't that long ago that we didn't have such gadgets. But the cold fact is that we have grown so accustomed to them that we now count on them. We need them.

Some might suggest that such dependence is weakness. I disagree. How is today's use of printers and copiers instead of carbons (which I started out using) a weakness? Or cast back even further. I'm sure ninety-five years ago the growing dependence on the automobile could have been seen as a weakness. But not now.

Clearly we should not be concerned with the increasing dependence of our law practice on machines and new gadgets. But we should be concerned with what kind of machine or gadget we have. Experience teaches that there are serious consequences to having the wrong device.

Let's use the car as an example. During an unfortunate stretch of my law practice I bought a minivan. It stripped me of my effectiveness as a trial lawyer, my self-esteem, and my ability to go faster than two miles per hour over the speed limit, regardless of what the limit was. If you happen to own a minivan

I hope you are not offended . . . but, of course, who cares what you think? Even if you are insulted, you won't say anything about it—you drive a minivan, for crying out loud! Driving to court in a minivan is like John Wayne riding into town on a cow.

I sold the minivan (yes, it's the one I shot . . . see the column "Traits: Being a Boss") and I bought a new pickup truck. My courtroom prowess returned, as did my pride, and my daughter was born less than a year later. Clearly we need to pay attention to the type of accessories we choose for our law practice.

And another thing: no discussion of lawyer accessories can leave out our computer systems. We at MehaffyWeber have gone with Dell (gotta support the Texas geeks). We have a Zoot 9000 system, complete with the Zapthebastards software package. I'll bet it's better than yours. If it's not I'll be miffed. It cost us about a billion dollars. They even had to bring in rented geeks just to train us. The system runs so flawlessly, we only need three full-time employees to keep it working. They are called "I.T." people. You can pick out I.T. people in any law office. They're the ones in the cone hats that have shining stars and crescent moons on them.

This system is amazing. It comes complete with firewalls, antivirus protection, and a "spam blocker." I'll bet it can block any other kind of potted meat, too. Without me doing a thing, it blocks all the stuff I don't need to see and only forty-one percent of the stuff I do.

With the right software it can do animations that make a head-on collision look like a Bugs Bunny cartoon. "No pain and suffering here, folks," I calmly suggest to the jurors as they watch their monitors. "Look. I can run it backwards. And look at my animated truck driver . . . why, he's the spitting image of Saint Christopher himself, the patron saint of all us travelers."

I'm telling you, folks, if you don't have the Zoot 9000 with Zapthebastards software, your opponents are going to whip the britches off you.

So get the right kind of accessories. And be thankful for all that these labor-saving and time-saving devices have done for us. With the right car, smartphone, and computer system at hand, success is assured.

BY LOU SCOFIELD

Nature of Practice: The Partnership

Summer 2009

Today's column is a very short piece. Just a note, really.

At the risk of insulting many of you, if you are a sole practitioner, you probably deserve to be, and this issue's topic may not be of real interest to you. But even if today you find yourself plying your trade alone, it is likely that you were, at least once in your past, a member of a partnership or firm, of some size or shape . . . so you still might find what follows to have some relevance. In this issue we address the law partnership.

The first definition I learned of a law partnership was that it is "Two who each have one hand so inextricably thrust into the pocket of the other that they cannot, without cooperation, plunder a third."

I'm not quite this cynical yet.

The definition and available forms of law partnerships and firms vary from state to state. Some are ordinary partnerships, some are LLPs, some are PCs, and some have other alphabets following their lofty names. The goals of the different forms are, however, universal: to glue together the players; to set out some rules; to share the take, along with the expense and overhead; and to, of course, limit liability to others.

Fortunately, the name of the partnership or firm is usually comprised of at least a couple of present or past lawyers. Recently I have seen some marketing types attempting to sneak in brand naming like "The Law Clinic." I hope this trend stops because, as you might imagine, the potential for abuse is rife: "Super Lawyers," "the Texas Hammer," "Husband Slashers" . . . you get the point.

But the value in being a member of a law firm or partnership goes well beyond the business benefits of name recognition. Shared expense allows you to buy actual books to accompany your computer. It allows you to hire actual secretaries and staff to assist you. And it allows you to have a nice place to go to do your craft (see the column "Traits: Your Office").

I advise that caution, however, be exercised in choosing with whom to join your law practice. You are known by the company you keep. A misanthrope for a partner will not only tarnish your reputation; you can expect a level of perfidy from such a partner to harm the internal workings of the firm as well. (I inserted this impressive vocabulary here to let my readers know that I have range.) In view of this, and the fact that we will spend more time with our law partners than with our spouses, it amazes me that we spend so little rational effort on the decision-making to join a partnership or to invite others to join.

Setting aside these concerns, I must say that the culture and relationships in a law firm can end up being the most rewarding parts of it all. Working with friends and those you respect is a real joy. Working with support and depth in lawyers, staff, and resources can add real force to benefit your clients. It is worth it, and a good firm is a blessing to its members. If these are not your feelings, please be referred back to sentence three, above.

Nature of Practice: Plaintiff or Defense, Part 1

Summer 2012

Defense lawyers and plaintiff lawyers—a defense lawyer's short book of thoughts on the choice.

Chapter One. To those who have decided at some point to be a courtroom lawyer, handling civil cases, on, of all things, the defense side, have you articulated to yourself why? It deserves a little thought (but I wouldn't spend the whole day on it . . . it doesn't deserve that much thought). My suspicion is that it simply happens to some. There you were, minding your own business, and someone up and offered you a job. It was a paying job. A job paying you more than you ever were paid before in your life. The rest is history.

Some of you will choose this course. Some inherit it by some chromosomal blip from a parent. Others arrive there after dabbling around in other areas of the law.

Chapter Two. A different question entirely is why you should stay in this practice on this side of the docket. That steady paycheck? Inertia?

I chose it, and stay in it, in part for the fun. It is a challenge, and often a complex one, to defend a professional liability case or a commercial case. But the real challenge is to defend a huge slobbery corporation against an injured plaintiff represented by a smart bearcat of a plaintiff's lawyer. The huge slobbery corporation is clearly the underdog. I like being the underdog. Sure, my client's checks are good, and we can afford to muster some pretty decent investigation, but to be given a fair shake by a jury of the plaintiff's peers is tough. (Not too many jury panels have a line of corporate executives and insurance adjusters populating the first couple of rows at voir dire.) Elevating the jurors to their oath, and holding them there, against the odds, is what defense lawyers do.

Our personal wit, charm, skill, knowledge of the law, credibility, experience, and flourish bring us victory more often than not, even in places designated as "judicial hellholes." And on those rare but unfortunate occasions that we get hammered . . . we still, of course, get paid.

What a life.

Chapter Three. But what if I became a plaintiff's lawyer? What if tomorrow I woke up as one? I stumble to the mirror and see there, looking back at me, some thinner guy, with slightly bouffant hair shaped a little like a preacher's. I get ready, go outside and hop into my tricked-out pickup truck, parked next to my third wife's Mercedes, and off I go to the local hospital. In the parking lot I put on my priest's collar and ease on up to the neuro ICU, trolling for accident victims.

Now, that's not fair! Hardly any plaintiff's lawyers are like that anymore. Most are very hard-working, honest, professional, ethical, skilled, and honorable people. And sometimes, yes, sometimes, they are even one of us, a defense lawyer with a plaintiff's case. Like Dustin Hoffman in Tootsie. Don't be ashamed. I've been there. At some time all defense lawyers have.

Chapter Four. If I'm a defense lawyer with a plaintiff's personal injury case, I do things different-ly than do many full-time plaintiffs' counsel. I treat insurance adjusters with respect, not disdain. I treat all doctors with respect, even if they don't deserve it, and even if I have to prove them wrong. I treat an opposing counsel (the defense lawyer) like I know and understand his innermost thoughts and problems . . . because I do.

In trial I start my closing argument discussing the damages issue . . . not the liability issues. I always start the same, with some version of the following: "My client here, Tom, woke up on a Thursday morn-ing and ate some oatmeal with his kids, Bobby and Wendy. He gathered a warm kiss from his wife, Polly, on the way out the door to his 1994 step-side truck. He drives to work and almost gets there, and would have, too, but for the defendant trucking company whose tired driver blew the red light and changed the lives of Tom and his family forever . . . and their damage from this is just starting. Let's begin with his medical bills . . . "

What? Remember, I'm a defense lawyer! I only take plaintiffs' cases that are laydowns on liability, with good damages and solvent defendants. Don't you?

Chapter Five: Kidding aside, I need to get a little preachy. Justice is best served when both sides of a case are presented in a professional, capable, and zealous way on behalf of our respective clients . . . in front of a jury. But powerful forces are at work gradually undermining the jury trial, and access to it as the arbiter of our disputes. To save the American jury trial is a fine calling for all of us, on either side.

Defense counsel groups and counterpart plaintiffs' organizations, as well as associations made up of lawyers from both sides of the docket, are working to save our juries

Every lawyer, every soon-to-be lawyer, and every citizen can help as well on an individual level. With every talk you give to civic organizations, schools, or other lawyers, regardless of the main topic, add a paragraph or point about the jury system. It will hold the attention of your audience because of its long history of success and importance in preserving liberty and resolving disputes. What a closed and unrecognizable place this will be if we lose the promise of a jury trial.

And how sad it will be to lose the contrast between defense lawyers and plaintiff lawyers. Not to mention the drop in hairspray and blow-dryer sales if the plaintiffs' Bar loses its identity.

Nature of Practice: Plaintiff or Defense, Part 2

Winter 2004

A war story from the defense side:

For many of us the side on the docket that we primarily occupy, the defense side, simply happened to us. For others it was a conscious decision, perhaps based on data-gathering and a legitimate decision-making process. Perhaps for you it was simply in your nature to become a defense lawyer, as opposed to a plaintiff's lawyer. In my case, I became a defense trial lawyer not only for the fun but because the defense gets to go second. I try to be ready by the second day of trial. I know that some of you higher-order thinkers will insist that such is not a legitimate reason for opting for the defense side of the docket. If you suggest I became a defense lawyer for the reason consistently attributed to us by others—the desire for the steady paycheck—I can promise you that such was not in my thinking when opting for this side. As many of you know, very little of my thinking reflects the type of maturity and responsibility that is shown in a person making their job decision based upon the potential for steady income.

Perhaps I chose it for the challenge. In many ways, ours is the more difficult task, and, in some ways, the more virtuous task, especially in personal injury cases. It is our job to elevate the jury to its oath to not let bias, prejudice, or sympathy affect their deliberations and findings in the case. Frequently it is the hope of the plaintiff's counsel that bias against corporations and sympathy in favor of injured plaintiffs will, in fact, carry the day. More often than not, it is the defense lawyer fighting to assure that the rules of evidence are followed rather than the whim of a particular judge. It is the defense side of the docket that turned the tide against the unqualified nonscientific testimony of professional "expert" witnesses. It is our side of the docket that more often than not is pressing for the application of common sense and reason, and against the conversion of our courts into a lottery for plaintiffs as well as their lawyers.

Of course, many defendants deserve to be unpopular, deserve to be sued, deserve to be held responsible in damages, and society is benefited by the threat of litigation leveling the playing field between those with little economic power and those with great economic power. But, of course, it doesn't work unless the law is applied fairly and damages held within the bounds of reason. It falls to us to see to it that fairness and reason prevail over the shotgun court, the biased jury, and those bearing false witness.

In light of this, allow me to suggest that the primary reason I became a defense lawyer, and have remained a defense lawyer, is because people are needed on the defense side.

A story: Years ago I watched my then-partner Dan Flatten (former ADTA president) try the Hardin case. It was a personal injury case where Mr. Hardin and a buddy (call him Jeff) were traveling up the Neches River at night when they collided with a barge owned by our client (call it "Dark Barge Inc"). The Neches River at night is a particularly dark and forbidding place, especially the cypress swamps on the east bank of the river. Except for a few places where dry land has managed to wrinkle or bulge a foot or two above the surroundings, the east bank is mainly a habitat for alligators and snakes. A meeting of alligators and snakes in human form was the destination of Hardin and Jeff. In particular, a paramilitary hate group was "training" that night and Jeff and Hardin were on their way, but did not manage to get to the festivities because of their collision with our client's barge.

The dispute involved the existence or sufficiency of lighting on the barge, and the injuries sustained by the plaintiffs. The only witnesses to the accident were the plaintiffs themselves. Their credibility was their case. They were represented by Joe Tonahill, a magnificent plaintiff's lawyer of the old school. Some of you will recognize his name. He and Melvin Belli defended Jack Ruby. Anyway, through the beginning of the trial, the court's rulings appeared to reflect the star-power of Tonahill. As the case wore on, however, the trial was handled fairly by the judge.

This brings me to the particular vignette worth remembering. Hardin and Jeff were lying. Their story about why they were on the river that night did not include their destination of their meeting of bigots. It was doubtful that they struck the barge. And their dramatic tale of collision and survival did not pass the smell test. But no specific impeachment was available; after all, they were the only witnesses.

During the cross-examination of Jeff, questioning turned to the location of lighting in the plaintiffs' boat. Of course the lighting on their boat was irrelevant to their claim that our client's barge was unlit, but Jeff did not know that. As Dan began interrogation on the point, Jeff showed a slight uncertainty. Sensing this, Dan approached the witness, practically crawled into the witness box with him, and exhibited to him a photograph of a boat similar to that which Jeff and Hardin had been using. "Now, where do you claim your light was?" Dan asked.

Jeff's eyes moved to the photo, to Hardin, to his lawyer, to the jury, and back to the photograph. For some reason known only to one who is lying, Jeff felt that the point was critical to his case. He fumbled at pointing first to one spot on the photo, then to another. Long pauses ensued between these inconsistencies and sweat literally formed on his forehead as Dan did not move from his perch beside the witness and patiently allowed him to "twist in the wind." To

Jeff time seemed to pass like a viscous river. Quietly, Dan looked over to the jury and then back at the photograph. Finally he returned to counsel table. Jeff was visibly relieved, but the damage had been done. Dan had not impeached the plaintiff with a prior inconsistent statement or the testimony of another witness. Neither was available. He had impeached the plaintiff with himself. Defense verdict.

Some years later Hardin made headlines (no pun intended) when his head was found in Louisiana, a significant distance from the rest of his body, which was found in Texas. I guess paramilitary pals react differently when pissed off than your typical bridge-club members. In any event, the demise of Mr. Hardin is, of course, not the point of the tale. The point of the tale is the example. There are sharp, brilliant lawyers among us, courtroom lawyers of the first stripe, such as Dan Flatten, who do the defense side for the best reason of all: because they are needed.

Traits:
Being a Boss

Winter 2002

I still remember the awkwardness of my first days as a lawyer. All was new and uncertain except my inflated self-image. Especially uncomfortable was the idea of telling a fellow employee, my secretary, to do something for me. I couldn't. The best I could muster was a request that she do something, and it amazed me every time she did.

I used to joke that I must be some sort of social communist at heart, unable to mentally honor a hierarchy. Of course, necessity, as always, won out. To be an effective team, a clear, undisputed decision-maker is needed. My first long-term secretary, Joyce (seventeen years), became that. I simply learned to do as I was told.

After twenty years with a senior partner in the firm, she came to me. Tired of his practice, she was interested in getting back to an active trial docket. At the time I was a star. I had run off an impressive string of courtroom triumphs, vanquishing foe after foe. (It mattered little that none had even six digits in controversy. One of my best dazzling efforts involved a dispute over $50.) So she came to work with me.

The turning point in our relationship came one day when she entered my office and closed the door behind her. She dropped a stack of unfinished bills on my desk and said, "You, Mr. Scofield, have to justify my salary." And she walked out. I did the bills.

I loved Joyce. She passed away. But when we were together we were a capable and formidable team . . . and seen that way by the legal community. Now I am blessed with another a great secretary, about whom I have no criticisms (and who, I might add, is typing this column).

Anyhow, experience teaches that the best lawyers are virtually always a result of a team. How do such effective relationships come about? Secrets and respect.

Secrets: Your secretary knows things about you, and you about her, that are kept secret. I shot my car on a hunting trip. (It was a minivan. It was an ill-advised purchase to start with. It deserved killin'.) Joyce learned of it when the body shop called to tell me it was ready and that before repair, they had photographed the wound to keep in their scrapbook. She kept it secret. See what I mean? Such things are bonding, if you'll pardon the pun.

Respect: The high-handed lawyer who treats his secretary like a worker, not respected as a thinking, feeling person, is not only less effective, but must enjoy life less as well. Mutual respect between "boss" and secretary seems a common theme among good lawyers.

This is not to say we never fall from grace. Being a "boss" is being human, too. But if, of late, you have been a jerk to your secretary, stop it. Remember the first attribute of your effective relationship. She knows your secrets. Now go and sin no more.

Traits: Respect for Judges and Civility

Spring 2016

The topic for this episode, dear readers, is judges. But it will take me a little time to get there, so be patient.

The other day I was returning home from Waco, Texas, by car. I was not on a freeway but on a regular U.S. highway. It was late at night and I was a long way from home. (Texas is a very big state . . . so big that they make iron skillets from its outline to sell to tourists. Yes, it's that big. So the Waco-to-Beaumont drive is a long one.)

Soon my mind was wandering with each little observation. I passed a sign at a bridge: "Mud Creek." Then a road sign: "Red Hill." Then another bridge sign: "Sand Creek." Straightforward, all-American names, simply call it what it is. Perfectly clear.

As these simple descriptive names contin-ued—"Clear Creek", etc.—I became a bit disturbed at the apparent lack of imagination of the folks who named these landmarks. Then my memory redeemed them. I remembered a bridge sign on Interstate 10, just west of Sequin, Texas: "Woman Hollering Creek." I kid you not. Perfectly ambiguous: is it describing what the creek is yelling, or what the woman is yelling?

Then, just as my musings on this sign were beginning, I saw an even more redeeming sign: one promoting "Kickapoo Creek," named after the Kickapoo Indians here in Texas. Not to be disrespectful, but to a guy whose mind tracks like mine, this is a very unfortunate name; to wit: why is it kick a poo? Because after you have kicked poo once, you're not inclined to repeat it?

That sign reminded me of another group of Original Americans, the Karankawa. Native to the coastal bend of Texas, the fierce Karankawa are reputed (unfairly, some have said) to have been cannibals. Now, folks, it is said that "a well-armed society is a polite society." If that's true, I presume people in a cannibalistic society must treat one another with unequaled civility. Ahem.

Speaking of civility, we are blessed that we still have the example of our courts, and the judges who preside over them, as guideposts for civility in our broader civilization. (See, I told you I would get to the topic of judges). Our laws, and the courts and judges we select as the focal point of their functioning (our civilized dispute-resolution forum), are the envy of the world.

Although the judiciary is not perfect, I, like all of you, have appeared before enough judges (from the brilliant and fair to the slow and biased) to know that the typical judge in America behaves much nearer the fair designation than the biased. Almost all strive to live up to their oath. Most understand the sacred burden of their public image and example. Few behave with overt bias, and fewer still engage in outright criminal behavior. As to the latter, the truly bad apples, when found, are almost always publicly shamed and stripped of their rank and freedom.

As for civility in the courtroom itself, the rules governing orderly trial, and our behavior in the courtroom, before our judges, are stylized and rigid for a reason. They vividly portray our reverence for the law. (The judge is entering: "All rise . . . ") There is nowhere else in our culture where we daily honor an institution from beginning to end with such civility, and this civility is contagious to all who are in court. It reflects our universal desire to hold something up as better, and higher than each of us individually stands.

The vast majority of our judges are inspired public servants, who earn much less than their talents could have brought them in private practice. Many feel isolated by their position. Of course, being a judge has its "perks," but to my mind, not enough to sit in their chair. I, for one, lack "judicial temperament," and delight in having a referee . . . especially one with a sense of humor.

Come to think of it, I have heard a pretty good judge joke: One afternoon in chambers, a lawyer was on the receiving end of repeated adverse rulings by the judge. The hearing concluded and as the disgruntled lawyer got to the door, he turned and asked the judge, "Your Honor, has anyone ever called you a dull-witted jackass?" Rising from his seat, the judge growled, "No!" "Then I shan't be the first," quipped the lawyer as he left.

So I have dragged you unwillingly through my musings on signs, which led to "civility," which led to judges, for the purpose of reminding you that we owe, every day, a debt of gratitude to these folks. The vast majority have brought honor to us, and themselves, and their positions. None were perfect, but no more broken than any of the rest of us.

Traits: Control

Winter 2005

I don't know about you, but I'm getting a bit tired of society referring to one of my best attributes as a malady. "Control freak" is the reference in the pejorative.

The desire to be in control is a professional asset for a courtroom lawyer. If a young lawyer is perfectly happy sitting "second chair" in a trial, that lawyer needs to be doing title searches, not trying cases. The courtroom counterpart of "Put me in, Coach" is "I'll take this witness."

Long before I ever uttered "I'll take this witness," I had exhibited the "control gene." Like young Mozart, I began mastering my craft in my youth, age five to be exact. Back then the words "control freak" were not juxtaposed unless as doctor's orders for a mental patient. Back then we were just called "bossy."

According to my bossy sister, I was very bossy. She should know; she was the cause. The story goes like this: It was the day I got my first bicycle. My sister and brother got theirs too. Off we rode down the street. As we approached a car parked at the curb, I was boxed in, so I instructed my sister to move over so I could go around. She didn't. I couldn't stop in time and hit the bumper of the car. The collision dented the front fender on my brand-new bike (bicycles had fenders back then). There was no damage to the car (I think back then they were made of recycled WWII tanks or something like that). Anyhow, my crumpled bicycle fender cried out to me every time I looked at it, which was every day, that I needed more control. Of course, I have never forgiven my sister.

When I reached the dubious age that qualified me to teach young lawyers, my most anxious task was letting them try the case. There I would sit, a figurative safety net, anguishing over my young charge's missed opportunities and bobbled objections. The good judges would ease the young lawyer through the main points, but some judges would send an occasional look my way that seemed to say, "Aren't you going to do something about this?" At least that was how I interpreted it, since in most cases I found it necessary to get to my feet at the critical moment. You know the rest: you clear your throat, go through the stylized ruse of introducing yourself to the court, then say some perfect thing that needed to be said, at that time, in that way, by you and no other.

Don't get me wrong, though. I know there are

those for whom the need to control all things, and people, around them reaches the level of a sickness. It's like an obsessive–compulsive compared to a mere compulsive person: a mere compulsive person would like all the pictures to be straight before leaving a room, while the obsessive–compulsive person can't leave the room until they are. The need to control is similar and can even be used to predict positions: people who enjoy controlling events are merely compulsive and are called "managing partner." They only get angry if you don't let them have their way. Obsessive controllers, however, become apoplectic if disrupted. We call them "judges."

Even just as a general proposition, it seems to me that it's good to be in control. It certainly reduces real risks of events that can be embarrassing. For example, it has been suggested to me that I should submit to hypnosis to help me quit smoking. I won't, of course, but not because I want to keep smoking. Rather, it's because hypnotists are known to plant things in your mind. I don't want to "wake up" from some post-hypnotic-suggested trance standing on counsel table with my thumbs in my armpits, flapping my elbows and quacking like a duck . . . just because opposing counsel accidentally said "chrysanthemum." Once the word got out (no pun intended) everyone would be using it against me, including my children. How can I take such a risk? Nope, no hypnosis for me.

Simply put, I don't see control as a problem. How can the desire to, one, reduce to a minimum "unknowns" and "uncertainties"; two, control the risks of a situation; and, three, insist on always being the driver, be an illness? The fact of the matter is that if I'm having surgery, I want my surgeon to be a "control freak." A serious hand-washing fetish would help too. I want my accountant to be so "anal" that he won't buy a calculator with an odd number of keys. By the same token, my clients should want a lawyer who will step up and do what needs to be done . . . himself or herself . . . not relying on others who may make a mistake . . . or be late . . . or screw it all up . . . or leave the room without straightening the pictures on the wall . . . sigh.

Traits: Courage

Summer 2004

This is The Bear Story. It begins innocently enough in the summer of 1974. Graduation from the University of Michigan with a starched B.S. in geology (and some nepotism à la my father) landed me a job as a field geologist with Mobil (now ExxonMobil). After a brief stay in Denver studying the geology of the Alaska Peninsula, I found myself on a 707 flying to Anchorage, with a party chief, John, and an aging geologist, Chuck. John had been to Alaska. Chuck had not. As a matter of fact, I came to later suspect that Chuck had never ventured further from his home than a short leash of urban domesticity would allow. En route John insisted I read a varied stack of torn-out magazine articles describing the grisly (if you'll pardon the pun) deaths of people in Alaska killed and eaten by bears. From the articles it appeared to me that the victims were always nature-loving photographers. They must be the tastiest of us. The worst of the tales described one corpse where the bear had merely disabled its victim before later returning to munch on him, alive.

So when Mobil issued us holstered .44 Magnum pistols, you can imagine the enthusiasm with which I determined to become a crack shot. I did not . . . for two reasons. First, shooting a .44 Magnum pistol is much like holding an ACME bomb in a Roadrunner cartoon. After the explosion and flame, you blink once and walk off camera with ears ringing. Hitting a target is out of the question. Aim, flinch, shoot, shake is the usual sequence. Second, John told me that if I shot a bear with a .44 it would only make him mad. If, in self-defense, we "really had to" shoot a bear, Mobil gave us a shotgun with some form of "Magnum" shell that supposedly would do the job . . . but only at point-blank range.

Equipped with these guns, large tents, food, and supplies, John, Chuck, and I were transported by float plane to a glacial lake on the Alaska Peninsula, literally two hundred miles from any other humans. There we set up camp in a small clearing. We were joined by a helicopter and its pilot/mechanic and for the next six weeks we embarked on the considerable task of locating and mapping "reservoir rock" for oil. In the wild, dangerous, and indescribable beauty of that place, we made and recorded our discoveries. We rarely saw any bears, and when we did we gave them wide berth.

When we were done, owing to the volume of our camp gear and the limited size of our floatplane, we had to break camp over two days. The first day we loaded the helicopter and airplane full as proverbial ticks, stuffed ourselves in as well, and flew to Homer, Alaska, for the night. We left behind considerable equipment and a standing tent. Our low rank elected Chuck and me to return the next day to complete the camp disassembly. The plan was to load the plane full. It would travel to Homer and unload while Chuck and I broke down the rest of camp. Then the plane would return for us and the last load.

That morning, as we circled the camp, preparing to land, we saw the damage. A bear had mauled much of the gear and had furiously dug holes at every place of food scent. But we saw no bear, so we landed and loaded the plane. As planned, Chuck and I stayed behind as the pilot taxied out to the center of the lake and struggled to get airborne under the load. Chuck and I stood there watching as a light, cold drizzle began to fall. Then we saw the bear. Our futile yells followed the plane as it lifted off. The pilot, being full of concentration on the task of flight, did not see our frantic waves. So there we stood, as the sound of the plane faded away, a useless urbanite and a frightened twenty-two-year-old, marooned in a small clearing with a huge Alaska brown bear at hand.

The bear had emerged from a brace of alders and watched us at a distance. I pulled my pistol and fired into the air. The blast did the trick. The bear moved back into the alders.

With this success, Chuck and I turned to completing the disassembly of camp. Because of the persistent drizzle we left the last tent standing, into which we stowed the remaining mauled and unmauled gear. We must have looked comical as we completed our work, constantly looking over our shoulders like overly cautious bandits.

Then there was nothing to do but wait. We did so inside the last tent. After a long while, and due in part to the incessant drizzle, nature called and I stepped outside the tent, found a spot, and was standing there in the midst of business when I saw movement. There, only one hundred feet away, ankle deep in the shallows of the lake, was the bear, looking at me.

Even in my youth I wasn't much at multitasking, so I'm sure I completed what I had started before I pulled the pistol and once again fired into the air. This time, though, the bear only blinked. I called to Chuck, "Bring out the shotgun, the bear is back."

After an unreasonable lapse of time, poor Chuck stumbled out of the tent. Somehow in the drizzle and quick call to action, his glasses had fogged. He looked for all the world like a confused wet hound as he wheeled about, nearly sightless, looking for the bear. By then I had decided some new noise might help. So I grabbed a shovel and began banging it on our propane tank (don't question the wisdom of this; it worked). Chuck quickly joined the effort and the cacophony forced the bear to retreat again into the scrub. But now I was truly afraid.

The drizzle deepened and drove us into the tent.

As we desperately listened for some sound of the airplane I reminded Chuck of the importance of the shotgun: the only thing we had that would stop a bear. As time oozed by, Chuck frequently looked out the tent flap. During one such lookout he suddenly groaned. "Oh no."

"On no," Chuck repeated. "He's coming this way!"

I told Chuck to get the shotgun, but Chuck did not move. "Oh no," he said again. Only this time he whispered it, frozen at the flap, looking to his right, watching there as our doom approached.

At that point I experienced a moment of clarity. Chuck couldn't save me and I did not want to be in a tent with a bear. I grabbed the shotgun, pushed by Chuck, and stepped out, looking to my right.

There he was. Twenty feet away. Right there on me. Two strides for a bear rush. A huge, top-of-the-food-chain predator. We both froze. He seemed surprised to see me. Then he stood up on his hind legs. Ten feet tall (OK, so he was only eight feet tall).

Calling on something I had read or heard, I waved the shotgun above my head to give the illusion of size. The bear seemed to study it. Thinking back now, I suspect he was looking me over for photography equipment. Seeing none, he moved his shoulders slightly, as if to turn away. In a snap something in me changed, and from the ages within us all, from somewhere deep in my DNA, from somewhere far back and primitive, came from my throat a strange, angry, fearful, guttural growl. In response, the bear turned and ran! No kidding! Full speed. With me chasing him.

As he crashed into the alders and disappeared among the thicket, I stopped at their edge, leveled the shotgun at the top of the scrub, and fired. I felt no recoil but I saw an explosion of shattering splinters and leaves fly up ahead, enhancing the effect of my pursuit.

I turned. There stood Chuck in front of the tent, open-mouthed. I walked directly to him, handed him the shotgun, and said, "Here. It's your turn." Then I retreated into the tent. To his credit, Chuck stood guard until the plane returned. The bear did not. To the astonished amusement of the pilot, we had not been killed.

True story, every word. Only my personal heroism has been enhanced by the sharper recollection provided by the passing decades. I am writing this on the thirtieth anniversary of those events. And what is the moral, the lesson for us all?

We all have our "bear story." Courtroom lawyers are a strange lot, but with many qualities in common. Some might suggest that courage is among those. Of course, courage may be nothing more than a willingness to do that which is necessary at the time. For a courtroom lawyer, such is not a bad quality, and, when coupled with blind luck, can yield considerable success.

Traits: Inflicting Our Practice on Our Children

Winter 2009

The teeth of an orthodontist's child are always straight.

So what sorts of traits do we big-shot courtroom lawyers inevitably visit on our children by virtue of this profession we have chosen? I have come to conclude that it depends, at least in part, on the nature of our practice. For example, in my early years my docket was comprised largely of car wreck, premises, and worker's compensation cases. Such was the typical "insurance defense" docket of a young Texas courtroom lawyer, and I had hundreds of such cases. Back then we "insurance defense" types were always either in trial or getting ready to try the next "whiplash," "slip-and-fall," or other "personal injury" case. As a consequence of the sheer number of these cases, and in my desire to protect my children from this dangerous world, I provided them with the tales of my relevant cases whenever I drove by the scene where one had occurred. An accident story could pop up and be inflicted upon them on virtually any trip, short or long.

To get an idea of what that was like, if you have been on a tram ride through a zoo, it was sort of like that for my boys. Except the zoo guide tells stories of how Wally the Wildebeest lived in perfect harmony with nature on the plains of Africa. My stories would have been more like: "Look over there, boys. That's where Wally the Wildebeest failed to watch where he was going, stepped on some moss, slipped into the moat, and drowned," or "Here is the lion enclosure, kids. Gary the Gazelle somehow got in there where he shouldn't have been, and that was that. They identified him from the only thing left, a piece of his nose . . . just enough tissue for the DNA test."

Yep, this is how it was for my boys growing up: "There was an accident at this intersection, boys, where the lady got tossed from her car and hit that fire hydrant over there," or "See that power pole over there, boys? A lineman got electrocuted up there and his belt held him in place. Then the EMT who was trying to get him down dropped him into that back yard, and the dog back there came and bit him . . . bad day all around for that guy." My poor sons grew up in a world where, for all they knew, there was carnage and death lurking literally around every corner.

There are some, I'm sure (probably psychologists and therapists), who would criticize my practice of inculcating the little ones with my tales of bloody outcomes of inattention or poor judgment. But what do they know? Most psychologists and therapists are so screwed up they make Freud look stable. Besides, I am convinced that all of us personal injury lawyers victimize our kids this way. We're just trying to give our children the benefit of our experiences in our profession. So what I've been doing all these years is perfectly "normal."

I don't think it's an issue for business lawyers, though. I can't imagine one driving his kid to the store with him, maybe to pick up granola bars and a box of Kleenex—with lotion already in it—saying, "See that house, Rodney? The lady that lived there died intestate and the IRS was going to stomp the snot out of her estate. Fortunately your old dad here had a few accounting principles up his sleeve, by golly, that saved her forty-two percent!"

See? It's just not the same as with us real lawyers.

I have to confess, though, that my behavior has changed a bit as the years have passed. Plus now my docket is primarily comprised of product liability and professional liability cases, and with this change, I don't seem to have the same desire to describe the people-munching qualities of products as I would have had with car wrecks and dangerous premises. Perhaps I have matured somewhat. I might once have considered putting yellow warning tape around the blender and other deadly gadgets in the kitchen or in the garage; I have stopped short of that, and merely preach caution.

I'm not too concerned about my new, less severe approach, either. It turns out that my past extrovert tales neither scarred nor scared my children as they should have. If they had, shouldn't my children be careful? Shouldn't their chosen fields or recreation reflect caution and a lifetime of their father pounding horror story upon horror story into their mushy little brains? Apparently it "didn't take." One son is a semi-professional SCUBA diver and instructor wanting to do commercial diving on oil rigs, and the other plans to apply for "demolition school" in the Navy . . . you know, disarming bombs, mines, and IEDs. Nope, I'm not kidding. If there is an activity box on a life-insurance application that, if checked, assures rejection of the applicant . . . my boys are into it.

Perhaps the travel stories they heard from me in their youth merely conditioned them to think that the risks they are now taking are by comparison benign. After all, they don't plan on being contributorily negligent like their dear old dad told them every last one of those plaintiffs was.

Besides, all orthodontists' children play ice hockey, don't they?

Traits: Reputation

Summer 2010

Now it is time to discuss the most important tool that we big-shot courtroom lawyers have in our considerable arsenals: reputation.

As I have grown older, I find that I am not only capable of doing less but am called upon to do less. No longer do I need to posture and snarl and paw the dirt to demonstrate my skill at these moves. My gray hair and furrowed face simply cry out to my opponents that I am fully able to posture, snarl, etc., along with the best of us. So from this lofty "guru spot" on the mountaintop, I feel quite comfortable in pontificating on this important topic. Here is what I learned after all this time:

It is never too soon to pay attention to your reputation. It is building with every moment of every day that you have practiced law. It comes from the totality of each trial, conversation, deposition, pleading, hearing, motion, assistance to the Bar . . . everything. It comes from how you behave in your personal life, spiritual life, and family life. It is the result of the totality of your behavior, talent, skill, and integrity.

Like a marble sculpture, your reputation can be the magnificent result of a thousand forming hammer blows, yet ruined by a single errant hit. Here I close my eyes and envision Michelangelo working on the statue of David. Along comes a pesky fly at which the artist, because of his unfortunate temper, strikes out . . . Suddenly the work of art is of an amputee . . . and considered by the snooty as a first baby step toward impressionism.

By the same token a reputation can be grievously damaged through no fault of the artist. Here I close my eyes and see Bart Simpson, the statue of David, and a can of spray paint . . .

Even so, a sound reputation can over time withstand attacks born of spite, jealousy, or mere opposition. And a sound reputation should be able to withstand the inevitable simple inaccuracies that will be spread about you. It is, however, doubtful that you will live down a reputation's shorthand: a nickname.

You cannot choose your nickname(s). You cannot give one to yourself. Over a nickname you have only limited control. It gets pasted on you, and sticks, if you bear even the remotest resemblance to it. Some nicknames are good. For example, there is a lawyer who shares my surname practicing across the border in Louisiana. His nickname is "Spike" Scofield. A great nickname for a railroad lawyer with a reputation to match its toughness. By comparison, I'm currently in a case with his lawyer son, and to separate the two "Scofields" in the case, the other lawyers have taken to referring to him as "Scofield the Bad" and to me as "Scofield the Good." I'd rather be "the Bad." Which demonstrates my point about not getting to pick your own nickname.

Now, back to the analogy of the marble sculpture that can be ruined by a single misstep. You need to guard your conduct carefully. It's not good enough to be honest, competent, moral, decent, smart, and professional most of the time. You are a lawyer. You have to be that way all of the time. I offer you here the sound observation I taught my sons: "You can spend your whole life obeying every law, ordinance, and even the most trivial of rules, yet you commit one little measly armed robbery, and wham, you're labeled a 'thief' for life." (How wonderful it must have been for my sons to have a father as sage as I?)

I have to confess, though, that these observations about reputation are not really mine alone. Will Rogers uttered the definitive standard: "Live in such a way that you would not be ashamed to sell your parrot to the town gossip." Similarly, my partner John Rienstra uttered this test for determining the ethics of conduct: "If you would be embarrassed to read about it in tomorrow's paper, don't do it." And in the Bible: Proverbs 22:1

In the end, if you are a careful, decent soul, your reputation should end up being a real asset to you.

Especially if you are known to be a tough, honest professional with a sense of humor, one who doesn't breathe his own fumes or believe his own publicity. Such a reputation will lead others to believe in you and make your job of persuasion much easier. And if, in some twist of fate, your reputation is somehow painfully harmed by an event, an ugly nickname, or your "fifteen minutes of fame," the damage may be permanent, but you'll still be, for the most part, a "piece of work" of your own making. Here I close my eyes and see the Venus de Milo.

Traits:
Your Office

Summer 2009

It is time we discussed our offices.

Being a good lawyer is not enough in this day and time of an oblique economy and stiff competition. We must look like good lawyers, too. And part of looking like a big-shot courtroom lawyer is residing in an appropriate office. And here, as in everything else I write to you about, there are a few rules.

First rule: Your office is not just a place to paint your name on the door and to put your desktop computer and landline telephone. It, like your clothes, needs to be impressive. If you are sitting at a crappy desk, in a crappy suit, in a ratty office like Philip Marlowe's, your client is not going to shell out $500 an hour for your stunning talents. No one really wants a "diamond in the rough" when their legal neck is in a noose . . . not at these prices.

So you need to get into the best office you can afford . . . and then decorate it appropriately. Mind you, I realize the physical plant limits you here. In the "old days" our offices were positively regal: spacious, with deep hand-set wood paneling; a separate sitting area with a small sofa, chairs, and coffee tables; elegantly appointed with art, lamps, vases, ashtrays; and with a liquor cabinet in the corner. The desk area had a large dark desk, inlaid with leather and matching leather wingback chairs. Law books were at hand behind the desk, and licenses were hung in custom frames, discreetly off to the side, but lighted and set so they would be seen. If this describes your office, congratulations, you're probably about to retire.

Today's office buildings of glass, steel, and lease rules limit your palette. But you can still use impressive furniture and hang your credentials on the wall. Which leads us to the second rule: display your credentials. You want your client to see that you were a "good student," that you "play well with others," and that you are "respected by your peers." So hang your credentials where they will be seen.

On the "good student" point, you want your clients to sit in your office, see your licenses and degrees, and think to themselves, "Say, he sure studied a lot; I'll bet he's really smart." They don't care if you were no fun back then. Every time I have had a body part removed by a surgeon, I did not want the doctor who could chug, tell jokes, and invent mischief in school. I wanted the guy opening me up to be the one who studied a lot and was really smart. I know it was a long time ago, and such distant academic applause means little, but you need to display all you can to elevate yourself, in your client's eyes, above the mundane no-fun human that you still are. Which is also why you display the other stuff, like the "plays well with others" credentials. And on the "respected by your peers" point, put up the gratitude plates and awards you have. The client will figure your deserve respect, at least to start with, if others have respected you. Besides, all these licenses, plaques, and awards can easily cover sloppy paint and wallpaper.

Third rule: Your general office décor should reflect your personality . . . not. If you think it should, you haven't been paying attention. The whole idea is to look respectable and worth $500 an hour. Trust me, as cool or as cute as your personality may be, it isn't what a new client (or even an old one) really wants to see. They want to see success. They want to see competence.

My own office is a perfect example. Above my credenza hangs behind me a very large painting by Dale Terbush. It is a powerful scene of a canyon through rugged mountains, with a brilliant, almost blinding sun dawning in the distance and a ribbon of river flowing far, far away, continuing its relentless erosion of the dramatic cliffs and peaks. In the foreground there are tough, gnarled trees that stand mute amid the rocks, and there is a coming storm off to one side. Folks, you could put Daffy Duck in front of this painting and he'd look competent.

The wall to my left is covered with "credentials"

(see second rule above). The wall to my right features a painting by George Boutwell. It's a Texas hill-country scene, with a farmhouse, a windmill, and an old pickup truck. It positively hums "Texas values." And in front of me, where my clients sit, is a small table separating two leather wingback chairs . . . and the leather matches the leather in my desktop. You guessed it—"tradition."

Lest you think I am completely manipulative, there are a few random hangings of paper Scotch-taped here and there that have lovely hearts and "I Love Daddy" drawn with Crayola. But in general, the above-described theme prevails.

Finally, fourth rule: Be tidy. No one likes to see a sloppy desk with piles of stuff, files, letters, paper clips, Post-its, and old documents that either should be in a file or should have been discarded years ago. As clients sit there and see it, they might start to think that some of the debris might be their case. I know it is form over substance, and sometimes a mess is unavoidable, but there have to be limits. I have a partner whose office is so messy that when he was out of town some creative friends of his did a movie about it. His office was the set, and the plot was that it could not be entered without full Hazmat suits, breathing apparatuses, and safety lines. That level of mess isn't good.

Related to the mess on your desk is the mess in your desk. Never keep old documents in your desk. No matter how useful they are to reminisce about, toss 'em. Tomorrow isn't promised to anyone, and potential personal mortification (in more ways than one) should be inspiration enough for you to keep the place free of old resolved grievance notices from the state Bar, denial letters from your E&O carrier, and, of course, love letters . . . which, it is said, "read great at the time, but always sound silly in court."

BY LOU SCOFIELD

Traits: Awards

Winter 2006

Allow me a moment of shameless self-promotion: I have just been named a "Texas Super Lawyer." Law and Politics and Texas Monthly magazines conduct a survey and publish a list of Texas Super Lawyers every year. (I trust the Texas delegation will not disclose to the rest of you how easily one becomes selected as a Super Lawyer.)

Since being notified of my new status as a Super Lawyer, I have been working on striking poses in front of the mirror. I quickly found that my experience in pose-striking was quite limited and I will probably need some professional help. I have also been shopping for a bodysuit with a large "S" emblazoned on the chest. I am hoping to find something light and stretchy. Not too garish, but cut in such a way as to flatter my Super Lawyer physique. Red seems to be the most popular color, but I can't seem to find my size . . . even on eBay. Why do you suppose that would be?

At one store I was posing in front of a mirror, when others began to look into the mirror at me. To me their eyes looked like those of a fish, with the comfortable stupor of ignorance, while powerful forces of nature, the seasons, solar system, galaxy, and universe, are at work all around. Before I became a Texas Super Lawyer I did not have such intrusive thoughts about others. Now I find myself victim of a creeping desire to use my remarkable powers to save everyone's undeserving neck. I am going to have to get over this. It's naturally reasonable to limit myself to saving only the necks of those who can pay. And now that I am a Super Lawyer, perhaps they should have to pay a lot . . . don't you think so?

Along these lines one runs into the "problem of superlatives." Like famous British under/overstatement ("The Battle of Britain was a bit of a scrape, you know . . . say, do you mind if I have another of those extraordinary scones?"), the use of the term "Super" to describe a defense lawyer runs the risk of not being taken seriously. It is important that this doesn't happen, and not just because serious regard for the label justifies higher fees. One of the real benefits of others believing you are Super is that the designation alone obviates the need to demonstrate one's super-ness. Think about it: you don't have to act tough or even ask an intelligent question of a witness if everyone in the courtroom knows you can melt ice sculptures from fifty feet using your vision alone. So now I am burdened with behaving in such a

way as to avoid bringing disgrace to the moniker Super.
I will maintain its dignity!

Of course, modesty constrains me to say that I
am not the Texas Super Lawyer, but rather a Super
Lawyer. It turns out that there are quite a few of
us, even though you haven't seen a lot of us flying
around. Setting aside the air-traffic-control concerns
that dozens of flying Super Lawyers would pose, there
are very good reasons for we Super Lawyers to avoid
calling attention to ourselves by crowding the skies.
Across the country the profession is engaged in a sub-
stantial push to enhance the image of lawyers and the
legal system. We are attempting to develop reasonable
restraints on some of the obnoxious advertising done
by some lawyers. It would be somewhat hypocriti-
cal to be flying in one's maroon leotard with taffeta
stripes and yellow lettering across the butt reading
"Super" on one cheek and "Lawyer" on the other . . .
all the while wagging one's finger in the face of some
other lawyer for calling himself "the Texas Hammer."

So I suppose snappy television ads are out of the
question. Besides, if I did advertise my Super status,
some aggressive lawyer would probably contend it
raised my standard of care.

For those of you who are not Texas Super Lawyers, and must satisfy yourself with membership in the
American College and ABOTA, don't worry. I am the
same humble courtroom lawyer I have always been.
At any Bar meeting you can comfortably approach me
and speak with me, and I will act as though I am just
as interested in you as I am in the other little people.

Travel

Spring 2016

One of the perks of "lawyering" is travel.

Although, with the passage of the years, some of the shine has worn off of traveling, when I first started I enjoyed virtually any trip out of the office. Even a drive up to Fred, Texas, to interview a witness was an adventure.

The charm is that there are always new people and new things to be found on a trip.

I especially enjoy flying. Often the soul in the seat next to me is more interested in sleep than chatting, so I honor their choice. But if chatting is an option, I'll do it. Some fellow travelers are simple, some complex; most are not famous, but all have a story to tell. For example, on a flight years ago, the woman in the next seat was both beautiful and engaging. It was easy to strike up a conversation. It turned out she was huge fan of horses, and I, having been a horse owner in the past, could relate to a limited degree.

But hers was a profound interest, involving a special focus on dressage, the execution by a trained horse of precision movements in response to bare- ly perceptible signals from its rider. (Don't worry, I didn't know what it was either, so my newly met traveling companion went to the trouble of patiently explaining it to me.) As you might imagine from the definition above, dressage requires a significant com- mitment of time, patience, and resources . . . and a really smart horse . . . which few in the world have. But she did. From that point on I learned of her pro- fession, family, hobbies, and other planned travels. Our conversation made the time pass quickly and after a couple of hours in flight we parted ways with the usual polite exchange of e-mail addresses.

That was many years ago, and we have not met since, but we are still in touch. We exchange photos and news about our work, events in our lives, and family. I always send her a copy of this column for ap- proval. I can't remember how that got started. I think her family was somehow connected with writing, or the movie industry, but somewhere along the way I decided she was in a position to judge entertainment, and could add an editorial touch. Now I just send it for fun. She says she enjoys it.

On another flight I sat next to a gentleman who was short, energetic, and as chatty as I am. He was heavily involved in the use of the new DNA technol- ogies to free wrongly convicted prisoners. He was consumed by his work and spoke with the zeal of a true crusader. Each tale he unfolded, of exoneration of a mistakenly or wrongly (they are not the same) convicted person, held the potential of a book of its own. The technical aspects of this work involve some detail, so I tossed in some thoughts and questions from time to time. Toward the end of the flight he asked my name, which I gave (yes, I gave my real name . . . can I go on now?), and he told me his: Barry Scheck. I related this meeting to my sister, Dr. Virginia Scofield, the immunologist and microbiologist (now deceased). Having some fame in her own right, she knew a lot on this subject. She also followed closely the public image of the science. She said Professor Scheck is running the Innocence Project to atone for his work and testimony contributing to the acquittal of O.J. Simpson in "the O.J. trial." I say even if her cynicism was well founded, he was certainly engaged in the Lord's work when I met him.

On another flight I actually took off from Chicago O'Hare Airport on time. For those who have not had the pleasure of flying in to or out of O'Hare, one never lands or departs on time. On one occasion, though, my plane quietly loaded passengers on time, pushed back from the gate, taxied to first position, and took off on time. On that flight I had a great conversation with the Continental Airlines vice president in charge of operations. Interestingly, the rest of the plane was full of Continental Airlines top brass (various vice presidents of everything) returning to Houston from a management meeting just before the

United Airlines merger. You don't suppose air-traffic control gave our flight preferential treatment, do you?

I'll spare you stories of the countless hairy landings, diverted landings, and otherwise unpleasant trips. No sense in reliving them. They are rare anyway. Instead I'll argue for this perspective: travel in the law practice is the necessary gift of variety, and variety expands your scope, imagination, and skills. If you swim around only in your own puddle you miss the reality and examples of countless people with different perspectives on life, born of different geography and subtle differences in culture. The transient meetings and partings occasioned by the traveling lawyer moving into and out of various jurisdictions give a special value to them precisely because they are abbreviated. Same for the acquaintances made on the plane.

And last, let us not forget, being able to fly great distances in a matter of hours is still a miracle. It also allows countless national societies and organizations to exist . . . so we can gather and reaffirm our commonality and rejoice in our differences. Plus, even if it did not serve this important purpose, the roar and raw speed of your jet taking off is worth the price of the ride.

Social Media

Summer 2004

I just got an e-mail advertisement that said: "Feeling depressed lately? You are not alone. Reply to us at ***.org," then referred a person to some place that helps lawyers with this problem. It is well meaning. But I read it as: "Feeling depressed lately? Welcome to the club! Just e-mail us and you'll drop into our data bank, at which time we will go all Julian Assange and everything and publish your name and/ or problems TO THE WHOLE WORLD . . . especially if your problem is sexy, or you have an unusual name, or you have an important job, or you make news later for some other reason . . . say like after an accident, or winning an award, or getting elected to an important office. If this happens, how can you complain? You brought it on yourself."

The advent of e-mails and now Twitter and

Facebook present problems for us that are important to consider. We all know to never write (or e-mail) anything that we don't want to see in court with an exhibit sticker on it (remember "love letters read great at the time, but sound silly in court"). But for some reason people are determined to be stupid in the use of Twitter and Facebook. Why would anyone want another human being to have so much power over them as is recklessly gifted to "friends" and strangers, in perpetuity, on these social websites? I want to ask these web users what my mom and dad used to ask me (more often than I care to remember): "What were you thinking?" Usually I wasn't. I was just being human.

So what is it about us humans that inspires us to reach out in this way? And don't tell me it is not in our very nature. We are doing it in an almost interstellar way. This very day we are sending signals into outer space attempting to make contact with other beings. Talk about talking to "strangers!" And how stunningly stupid is that? Any beings capable of responding to our "tweets" into space could also be capable of interstellar travel and will have no trouble destroying all of us in a week. They would be so far in advance of us in technology, communications, and culture that we will be goners for sure.

I'm reminded of the story of the boy who found an injured bird on a very cold winter day. But, having his hands full, he could not immediately carry it home. So he placed the bird in a warm, fresh pile of cow manure with the plan that he would go home, put down his load, and return. Meantime the bird, feeling warmer and better, began to sing. A fox heard him, and came and ate him. The moral of the story is: if you are up to your neck in it, keep your mouth shut.

Sound advice for humanity. What makes us think that "aliens from another place in space," massively ahead of us, will be benevolent and not simply come, kill us all, and take our pleasant planet for their own? Why are we "singing" out to them? Because, you say, we humans are so decent ourselves that they will be kind to us? Are you kidding? Look what happens when cultures clash on our own planet. Ask the natives in both North and South America how it worked out for them when Europeans discovered them. And their culture, communications, and technology were only slightly less advanced than the Europeans', compared to the degree of advancement the "interstellar aliens" will have over us. To me it is simple. We are very unwise to be sending signals to the stars, and only slightly less so to be posting our lives on the Internet "social" sites.

Look at it another way. The folks who invent, run, and are proficient at this computerized world have a lot more time, motivation, and knowledge than you on how to maximize, for their benefit, use of your information. In a very real sense, they are your technological superiors, and, believe me, they know they are. They also know it would take you significant dedicated time and effort to try to use existing laws to stop them from doing whatever they want with your personal data, and that you likely won't ever try to stop them . . . even if you had a right to claim your privacy, which you probably don't. So once the information on you is out there, that's it. As with a tattoo that seemed like a good idea at the time, you are stuck with it. Only with a lot of money and pain can you clean it off, and even then it always leaves a scar.

So why is it in our nature to expose our personal information in the face of cautions against it? I'll tell you why. But because I'm too lazy to actually research the phenomenon in learned writings from respected psychologists, I'll just tell you what I think: like the children we are, we want attention, we want to feel important, and we want to be accepted as part of a group. Most of the time posting our personal information doesn't immediately backfire, so we take the chance.

Anyway, that's what I think explains it.

Even so, our children's life expectancies will be one hundred. That is a long time for a data bank to be working you over. So my advice is not to give the social "webworld" the data to start with.

As lawyers we need to be routinely advising our clients to avoid the social "webworld" unless they have a person hired and dedicated to maintain it, keep the cranks out of it, and continually purge the baseless critical attacks and libel. This full-time monitor will have to be vigilant. Was it Jonathan Swift or Mark Twain who observed that a lie races halfway around the world before the truth can pull on its boots? Better to just stay out of the social "webworld."

And as lawyers, we need to take advantage of the foolishness of others by researching on the Internet the other party, witnesses, and potential jurors. As most of you already know, there is a wealth of information now out there.

Finally, as parents we need to urge our kids to stay out of "webworld" and to socialize the old-fashioned way. If they resist, you can tell them the story of the bird. Then spend the next twenty minutes trying to explain to them how it applies to the point.

BY LOU SCOFIELD

Accuracy: Is it Correct?

Summer 2007

If we knew half of what we think we know we'd be brilliant. Unfortunately we don't. Accordingly, it is an important discipline for attorneys to continually question themselves (regarding a fact, the law, their opinion): "Is it correct?"

Alas, dear victims—er, I mean readers—I once again will be abusing this forum called A Word From Lou to impose upon you my personal opinion about something (hint: see introductory sentence above). And, as usual, it will take me a while to get to the point. So just bear with me. Let's start by considering the climate.

I am in favor of the climate, whatever it is. Hotter, colder, whatever it decides to be is fine with me. If asked to vote, I'd vote for global warming. Again, not because I'm against global cooling or global staying-the-same-ing, but because I'm for warming. If it gets warm enough and an Al Gore—magnitude sea-level rise occurs, my home, which is twenty-three feet above current sea levels, will be desirable beachfront property.

Unfortunately, I have no confidence in the predicted consequences of global warming (whether or not it is caused, or contributed to, by man), because everyone on every side of the global-warming debate doesn't know what they are talking about. They all made it up. Not a one could hold up under a light Daubert challenge.

Take the former vice president for example. He suggests in an acclaimed, Academy Award–winning film that the earth is warming, true . . . and that people are a big cause of it—true or not, he (and others) made this part up. The former vice president doesn't know anything more about global warming than you do. Think about it. If you were going to hire someone to survey available studies, gather the data, and give you a definitive opinion, based on current knowledge, on whether people are causing the warming of the earth, would you hire a law-school dropout with an undergraduate degree in government?

But then again, a lot of folks end up giving right answers for the wrong reasons . . . at least half my jury verdicts, I suspect. So Vice President Gore may be right (though he has no reason to believe that he is). Indeed, it seems the folks who are now affectionately called "global-warming deniers" are just as short of facts, if not as short of credentials, as the former vice president.

The reality is that the earth is warming and has been since before we were children. In our lifetimes we have watched it. As a geologist (B.S. Geology/ Mineralogy, University of Michigan, '74) I've studied it and its effects on the retreating glaciers, erosion, and depositional environments. I watch the reports like you do: ice cores show lots of warm and cold spells with warming preceding increased atmospheric carbon dioxide. Not the other way around. Computer models show carbon dioxide and especially methane are greenhouse gases, sure to trap heat. Is one the cause and one the effect, or are both causes? We have no data to tell us which answer to choose. Plus, powerful data shows rainfall trumps it all, and we have no idea how much it rains on earth in any given year. Even close study of the subject, using current data, refuses to show whether we play a part in it and, if at all, how much or how little.

The planet has warmed and cooled countless times before, with variability and extremes far in excess of that experienced today, and we know no more about the cause of these cycles than about the cause of the current cycle. I'm open to supporting research into the countless potential causes. The correct answer could be very important to us. Unfortunately, the climate warriors of today are not open to other ideas about "climate change," and this makes for an entertaining fight.

Isn't it fun watching the fight?

I love watching this fight. It's like an argument in a bar where neither drunk can express himself correctly, and neither will be convinced by the other, even if one of them does have the facts. It also reminds me of an exhibit that was (and might still be) at the Field Museum in Chicago. The Field Museum is a science and educational museum containing among its exhibits paleontology displays, dinosaur bones, and cool information about the time of dinosaurs. Of late a debate has arisen among folks who study this stuff about whether dinosaurs were warm-blooded creatures or cold-blooded reptiles. So the museum has a place where visitors can vote: warm-blooded or cold-blooded. When I voted, the cold-blooded total was beating the warm-blooded vote, two to one. Of course, such a poll is useless: the voters are clueless of the truth; the truth is not known, and may not be currently knowable; and if cold-blooded wins the vote, it will have no effect on whether dinosaurs were, in fact, cold-blooded. Simply put, the voting poll on the topic is useless . . . but is it? After all, it gives us the illusion of knowledge.

The drunk in the bar can display this poll result as support for his claim that dinosaurs were cold-blooded. Why not? Sober newscasters cite poll results from public samplings every day, where those questioned are just as ignorant as the museum voters. This type of fake information is everywhere. In the 1970s nutritionists almost killed the breakfast-cereal industry claiming cereals were just empty calories. Today's data says otherwise. Enhanced breasts were mercilessly attacked by the "junk science" attacking silicone. The Alar apple scare, just about anything

Freud ever said or wrote about the human mind, any economist's prediction, "stress" causing ulcers, . . . (wrong, wrong, wrong, wrong) . . . are just a few examples of the illusion of knowledge, where folks earnestly believed something because they heard it in the public square and a consensus at least temporarily formed around a given "fact," only for it to later be disproved.

Unfortunately, pressing your point based on consensus and not considered judgment sometimes does harm. I'm thinking here of the ninety-four "intelligent" Duke faculty members who signed the petition that presumed the guilt of the Duke lacrosse players.

Of course there is such a thing as being right, and knowing the truth. Why, just the other day Galileo was telling me that the whole time he was prostrating himself before the Catholic Church and denying his theory of the solar system, he had his fingers crossed. He said, "Truth, especially scientific truth, is pesky. It will eventually come out."

So it will be with determining the cause of global warming. Some day we will know the pesky truth. (It's probably caused by something we haven't thought of yet. Maybe the culprit is CO2 from carbonated beverages, like beer and soft drinks, in which case we will just have to get used to the Earth being hotter). In the meantime, fortunately, the global-warming debate will continue to fill slow news days. Our ignorance and certainty in it will compel us to flail about, spend billions on remedies that won't work, divert resources from truly life-saving human endeavors, and inspire our inventive spirit to come up with stuff that will let us live quite comfortably with climate change, regardless of what causes it.

It seems to me that the only way we'll miss enjoying this unfolding ridiculous argument is if we recognize, then admit, that much of what we "know" is the illusion of knowledge, mere constructs to avoid uncertainty. If we admit we don't know even half of what we think we do, our pride may diminish and we may stop yelling at each other. Now, what's the fun in that?

BY LOU SCOFIELD

The System: Pet Peeves

Winter 2010

I don't like it when I do or say stupid things. But I forgive myself.

For some reason, though, I have a hard time forgiving some of the stupid things others do or say. A mature response on my part would involve tolerance, Judeo-Christian forgiveness, and the common sense not to waste my time on the ridiculous. But, dear readers, as you know from your past visits to this column, I have none of these attributes. And as usual I am going to impose my thoughts upon you.

I am bothered every time a business or service advertises its "combined years of experience." I've seen an ad on television where a law firm promoted itself as having fifty years of combined legal experience. That is just stupid. Don't slow me down . . . these advertising people are stupid. I know of a kindergarten class with twenty-five five-year-olds who, upon completing the year, will have twenty-five years of "combined academic experience." That is much more than it took most of us to get through school. Even so, I am not going to sit in one of those tiny chairs, shove little Mimi's pile of blocks aside, and ask her to compare George Berkeley to John Locke and David Hume.

By the logic of "combined experience" there are some very large law firms that numerically have more than two thousand years of combined legal experience . . . easily enough to take them back to the time that the Lord was walking among us. Now that's impressive, eh? How exactly does two thousand years of combined legal experience work? I know the rule against perpetuities is slightly complex, but even I wouldn't need more than 1100 or 1200 years of experience to understand it.

Anyhow, you get my point. It is stupid to tout one's competence by such a standard. While partners, associates, and support staff are a huge help to us all, when you get down to it, the experience and talents of the single lawyer is what the client, rationally, looks to. Along these lines falls a tale from back when the large "mega firms" were just getting started.

In the 1970s Fulbright & Jaworski was considered one of the biggest firms, with roughly two hundred fifty lawyers. One of its attorneys appeared at a hearing where the judge was scheduling further hearings. The attending lawyer advised the court that he would not be available for the selected future date.

To this the judge responded, "You have two hundred fifty lawyers there at Fulbright. Get someone to cover it for you." The Fulbright lawyer brightly replied, "Yes, Judge, we are two hundred fifty wide, but unfortunately we are only one deep."

Another thing that bothers me is that George Orwell's Animal Farm is not required reading for everyone that works for the government. Although I must admit I am fearful that most of the readers would view it as a how-to book, rather than political satire. If I were running the world, I would make every one of those feather-bedding politicians and intractable bureaucrats not only read the book, but take a test at the end. If they failed the test they wouldn't lose their job (no one in government ever loses their job) but would be reassigned to the Louisiana Gulf Coast and required to use their hair to sop up excess oil from the BP oil spill.

Excessive? Perhaps, but this ranting and venting on my part is already making me feel better.

Another thing that bothers me is the way we are passively allowing the civil jury trial to be taken from us. Talk about stupid: allowing this is really stupid. Yet time and again legislators are precluding civil liability and substituting administrative remedies for dispute resolution. On top of that, it is now commonplace for sellers of goods and services to insert arbitration clauses in consumer contracts . . . and they are being enforced. Setting aside the implications that this has for freedom, and the fair administration of justice, it isn't much fun. As for me, I will take the combined intelligence of twelve jurors over three arbitrators, any day. (I know, I know. My reverence for the jury's "combined intelligence" seems inconsistent with my rant against "combined experience." It isn't. See how easy it was to dispatch your incredulity?)

And that reminds me of one more thing that bothers me. Since when is consistency such a virtue? Since we first communicated, people have had the recognized right to change their minds: "Chase the mammoth! Spear the mammoth! . . . Er . . . Run away! Flee the mammoth!" See?

Even so, a day does not go by without some television show, newspaper, or other form of media trotting out some video or recording of a past statement made by a public figure that is now completely (or at least "apparently") contradictory to that person's current position. This "Aha!" or "Gotcha!" doesn't prove anything. Whether you are liberal or conservative, being "caught" with some statement from your past should not make a hill of beans. What is important is whether, after growth and consideration, the position you are expressing now is correct. If you are now correct, I applaud your conversion. If your changed position is now wrong, shame on you. But it is no more "wrong" if you happen to have been right in the past than if you have always been wrong. It is, simply, wrong.

So this gloating over inconsistency should stop.

Though I agree consistency in accurate and honest speech is a virtue, consistency in inaccurate and dishonest speech is not. And this ridiculous attention to prior inconsistent opinions holds the threat of chilling a person's willingness to adopt a better but different position, for fear of being excoriated merely for the change. Reasonable flexibility is lost.

Sigh . . . but such excoriation is too tempting for the media to stop doing it. In view of this I request that each of you, upon completing your reading of this article, gently tear it from the other pages, chew it up, and swallow it, so it cannot be used against me in the future.

The System: News Media

Winter 2011

I do not watch shows or movies about courtroom lawyers. I have watched enough of them in the past to know that, with only three notable exceptions, they are all crap. The exceptions are movies, all in black and white. We courtroom lawyers don't look right in Technicolor. All of you know which movies are the three exceptions. Hint: one starred James Stewart, another Gregory Peck, and the third Charles Laughton.

Now to the point: unless you can look and act like one of those three characters (and you can't), you have no business ever showing up on the TV screen. More generally, you have no business showing up in any form of the news or entertainment media.

And when dealing with the media on a high-profile case, don't.

Whenever I see a trial lawyer mugging it up for

the cameras on some "fifteen minutes of fame" case, I am reminded of someone's observation about UFOs: the samples of humanity the space aliens choose to capture and "probe" always seem to be folks with marginal brainpower and a limited number of teeth. If aliens form their impressions of us from this sampling, we are all in trouble. Likewise for the image of lawyers, as gleaned by the public from seeing our publicity hunters.

The simple truth is that a jury trial, while in progress (in the context of the law being applied, by a judge with a history, before a jury unique to the case, between personalities, varied legal talents, and nuance), is much too complex, legally, factually, emotionally, and contextually, to be accurately reported in an evening newscast, a morning paper column, or a rapid-fire tweet or blog. (Whew! Now THAT is a sentence! Did you get all that? Go back and read it again.)

So my advice is not to talk to the media. In the few "high-profile" cases I have handled I avoided the media entirely. Even then, on one occasion, I had statements attributed to me by a Wall Street Journal reporter that I had not made. (I considered chewing out the reporter, then remembered the old saw: "Never get into an argument with someone who buys ink by the barrel." I dropped it.)

There are several theories about why, in trial coverage, inaccurate reporting is the rule. One theory is expressed in the run-on sentence above, having to do with the complex nature of the jury trial itself. Another theory has to do with the widespread belief that objectivity in reporting is gone, and all reporters now have an agenda. I prefer a third theory embodied in another old saw: "Never attribute to malice that which can be reasonably explained by stupidity."

In my experience, inaccurate reporting springs from the fact that journalists for the most part are neither lawyers by training nor the brightest Crayolas in the box. Most do not understand the law. Some do understand the process, but not the reasoning behind it. So when they report about it, they are to some degree always wrong. The result, regrettably, is that the impression the public comes away with is jaded.

Too critical of journalists? Well, when was the last time you heard a reporter caution his audience: "What the lawyers say about their case can't be complete, because they, by rule, are precluded from telling the press information that is privileged, or information that the lawyer knows will harm his client. Such withheld information could drastically change your view of the case"? When was the last time you heard a reporter explain to her audience: "The adversary system is the best to get to the truth, and works best only if both sides cast the case in a light most favorable to his or her client"? When was the last time you heard a reporter say: "Daily press coverage of a trial in process is irresponsible . . . You viewers should wait until each side has had its turn, and all of the evidence, argument, and court rulings are in. Only then will this reporter finally have the full picture, and be able to fairly report on the matter"? And when was the last time you heard a journalist begin a segment on some high-profile case by reminding the audience of the latest half-dozen times their speculations involving some other poor souls turned out to be completely wrong?

You won't ever hear reporters disclose such things. So the damage done to the public trust in jury trials will continue due to inaccurate reporting.

But journalists don't deserve all of the blame. They have accomplices: lawyers. Shame on those publicity hounds who stand before the cameras trying to gain publicity, or reputation, and spin the coverage. And shame on those who try to poison the jury pool with pretrial posturing and information "leaks." Gag orders should never be necessary, but are, to control the media mouths of licensed lawyers. By contrast, I seem to recall a time when it was considered unethical for a lawyer to make a personal attestation of the guilt or innocence of a client. Now it's common for the lawyers on both sides of criminal and civil cases to personally pitch for their clients, as though the lawyer's personal beliefs should have any relevance at all.

Ah yes, dear readers, as you can see from the foregoing it has come to the point that your humble author has reached "geezer status" . . . lamenting the loss of the good old days.

Barring a return to such idyllic times, I have some advice for you on dealing with the press . . . other than "don't": If a statement is absolutely unavoidable, do it in the form of a press release, and run it by your partners before you send it out. In it, do not address the substance of the case. Instead remind the press that the judicial process is a serious and honored institution. Remind the reporters that they too would hope to be treated fairly if they, or their children, were involved. That in our free land neither the press nor the public can appoint themselves judge and jury. Instead we have entrusted that solemn duty to the court and the chosen jury. Express confidence that if the press holds itself accountable to protect this precious truth, the case will run its course and both sides will have a chance at the fair trial both sides deserve. But if the press does not, and instead goes twisting off into speculation, you hope someday the same media feeding frenzy pecks out their . . . (er, better leave this last sentence out).

I must always remember that if the press were only free to write "approved" material, and were not free to be stupid, none of us would be free. Still and all, when it comes to courthouse coverage, I wish the media had better judgment, that the lawyers would gag themselves, and that all news clips on trials were required to be in black and white.

BY LOU SCOFIELD

The System:
A Higher Calling

Summer 2014

When my daughter was about nine years old I decided it would be a good time to take her to see our nation's Capitol. To expand the adventure, I arranged for the trip to be by passenger train from New Orleans to Washington, D.C., and back again.

First-class accommodations aboard the Crescent seemed appropriate, since it would give us more space, our own bathroom, and a shower. So we were set.

On the appointed day we stepped from our house in the hamlet of Beaumont, Texas, uttered, "A journey of a thousand miles begins with a single step," and drove the four-hour trek east to New Orleans. It was a familiar beginning for us. As with my sons before her, I had been dragging my daughter around this great land on various "grand adventures" since she was five, and New Orleans had been a prior destination. We spent the night in the Windsor Court, which had been the finest five-diamond hotel in New Orleans. But this time it was after Hurricane Katrina, and though more than a year had passed, half the hotel floors were closed, and even the suites on the open floors still showed considerable damage: sad disrepair, and a grim tribute to the power of nature.

Early the next morning we went to the train station, presented our credentials, and were directed to our car and "first-class" cabin. Now, for those of you who have not ridden a passenger train in the U.S., or have not done so lately, be advised that Amtrak is not like European train service. The car we were in was built in an era when the biomass of people was much smaller than today. I have no idea how Hitchcock filmed North by Northwest in such a confined space. Our room was tiny, and it was the biggest! They issued cans of butter for the other passengers so they could lube their hips in order to fit into their cabins. You might expect the color scheme to have been bright in order to offset the cramped circumstance. Nah, it was grey. The color palette must have been chosen by a person who despised trains and/or his parents, or chosen by a schnauzer, or someone in the Army Air Corps in 1943.

I don't want to sound like a complainer (which, of course, I am) but our private bathroom and shower was nothing like the literature suggested. Imagine the restroom on a Boeing 737. Now make it narrower. Put a drain in the floor. Hang a hose on a wall hook, and presto!: you have a shower above the toilet. If you dropped the soap you would have to open the door into the cabin, back out, caboose first, then bend to pick it up . . . Even so, I assure you it was a lot better having it than not having it.

Then there was the track over which we rattled and swayed and jerked. No Swiss engineering and maintenance here. It was akin to being in the North Sea, in a winter storm, on a small fishing boat. Walking from our car to the dining car was not easy. Like Carmen Miranda's skirt, if you weren't holding on to something at all times, you were lost.

Yet my nine-year-old companion loved it all, and she especially loved visiting with our fellow passengers. Then the day, and sights that rolled by, led to night. That night I almost got some sleep. When we arrived in D.C. the next morning I thanked our hosts, went to the Amtrak desk, and canceled the train trip home. Air travel home seemed wiser.

In D.C. we saw the Lincoln Memorial, the Washington Monument, the Capitol, the Smithsonian, and the White House, and my daughter saw her first "crazy man" . . . literally. (I know. Get it out of your system—"crazy man other than her father." Feel better? Can I go on now?) He was a lost soul prone to yelling at strangers, some sort of protest about which his enthusiasm never waned. We crossed to the other side of the street.

Presently we found ourselves in Arlington National Cemetery. I had been to Washington, D.C., a number of times but had never gotten there. Our spring day there was bright and cool, and we almost had the place to ourselves. Using a map, in steady sequence we walked from monument to place. We paused at what we tourists call the Tomb of the Unknown Soldier and watched as they changed the guard. Just a few steps from this is an amphitheater, a beautiful place on its own, built entirely of spotless white marble, the shaded parts of which, when touched, felt impossibly cold. As we continued our walk on the paved paths we looked across the row upon row upon row of markers. The sheer number of these is difficult to take in, much less comprehend. There is a weight in that place that steadily builds on your heart: all these people who gave their lives, short or long, in service to their country, in service to us.

Then the general became the specific. As we walked the path through a small wood and approached a stone road, we came upon a lone man, a bugler, standing off in the trees. A moment later a man with bagpipes took up a position in the woods off to the bugler's right. We proceeded across the road and as we did we heard the footfall of slowly approaching horses. We moved a respectful distance away, turned, and watched as the honor guard quietly rounded a curve in the road. They were crisp, clean, precise, and serious. Behind them moved a horse-drawn wagon with a flag-draped coffin, and behind it was led a riderless horse. Trailing was a silent group of two dozen loved ones and friends, all in funeral black mixed with small shocks of the white from shirts and blouses. And with this procession came a vivid, palpable sadness felt even by my daughter and me, total strangers, standing in honor at a distance. This seemed no celebration of the life of the deceased. This seemed a moment of terrible loss.

It was woven like a perfect fabric: the bagpipes and "Amazing Grace," the procession, the words, the guns fired in salute, the bugler's "Taps," the flag given to the seated woman with the whispered words "on behalf of a grateful nation."

Earlier, when the procession was stopping, the horse pulling the wagon had slipped on the rocks and slope of the road, but had steadied perfectly, and halted. It did its job.

I think back on this trip, but not often enough. It serves as a reminder that you and I have chosen a higher calling. Years ago each of us promised to be the protectors and practitioners of the system and laws that have served our nation, and helped protect our freedom, for over two centuries. Though much of our work is mundane and thankless, each day it is done right it serves to fulfill that promise. Arlington and that funeral are symbols of the accomplished duty and sacrifice of others for this freedom. If we forget, shame on us.

Tips:
Groveling

Winter 2003

Historical note: This article was written during the long aftermath of the ENRON collapse. On December 2, 2001, ENRON declared bankruptcy. In the very short period leading to this declaration the company went from being a high-flyer to complete collapse. It was a surprise to almost everyone, and its accounting practices were sharply criticized, to say the least. Many of the top brass at ENRON were in big trouble. The work of its outside accounting firm, Arthur Andersen, was also criticized and Andersen was found guilty of illegally destroying documents relevant to the SEC investigation of ENRON. That conviction was later overturned, but by then Andersen was also out of business.

The other day I was standing at the firm's Arthur Andersen machine, shredding personal documents . . .

ahem . . . and ruminating about how such a respected and venerable firm as Arthur Andersen came to fall so far from grace. There must be something about ruminating while shredding that yields insight, for it came to me that arrogance must have been a cause. "Pride goeth before the fall" is the wise old expression of the concept. How else can we explain the remarkable blindness of such smart people?

How are they going to get out of this seemingly impossible pickle?

I recommend groveling. Mind you, I doubt that accountants are invested with the skill necessary to effectively grovel, and likely are still too proud to authorize effective groveling on their behalf. It may be necessary, therefore, to hold a few sacrificial accountants into the air as dart catchers to convince the others to cooperate. Still, it's the ticket, enlightened groveling.

Speaking of groveling, why isn't effective groveling taught in law school? Why don't we see groveling honored in seminar, song, or history? Perhaps it is because groveling . . . effective groveling . . . is a rare talent and, being a talent, it is very difficult to teach. Even so, it is often needed and should be respected. Groveling is best observed and appreciated in the most stressful of circumstances—when all is on the line, the walls are crashing down, and no escape seems possible. At such magical nexus points, the talented will step forward with the ultimate groveling skills of the true trial lawyer.

I'm not talking about begging or pleading here. That's just embarrassing to the lawyer and the observer. And there are those who view the art in only the basest sense, as evidenced by the statement "Of course I know how to grovel; I'm married." Such a crass, simplistic view is inapposite. We're talking true groveling here. Examples:

Co-optive groveling: "Could you save me some postage, Judge, and send a copy of your order to my malpractice carrier?"

Personal groveling: "Well, if that's your ruling, Judge, I can always go back to teaching freshman English at the community college."

Giving-a-hint groveling: "You know, Judge, if you were to find my client was incompetent for two months, limitations will not have run."

Sarcastic groveling: "Judge, this is excellent. Without my witnesses this trial will go a lot faster."

Feigned-innocence groveling: "Violated what motion in limine?"

I am sure the list of examples is endless. I am just as sure that this talent is among those that separate the truly wonderful attorneys from those who are merely very good. Naturally there are myriad other talents that make for a wonderful attorney, such as the ability "to see the freight train coming" and the like. But groveling has a special place in the quiver that holds the arrows that are the tools of the capable trial lawyer. And my instincts tell me that Arthur Andersen could really use a lawyer with such a talent.

By way of epilogue, as with so many lessons that we are called upon to pass along to each new generation, we must be mindful to communicate to each new generation the significance and necessity of using the talent of groveling, and the ability to distinguish it from other behaviors. I can hear myself now, after a tough but successful hearing, patiently explaining to a young associate: "That, my impressionable charge, was groveling; it only looked like ass-kissing."

Tips: Negotiating

Winter 2012

Now that we are all successful, smart, and reasonably well respected in most circles (by everyone except for the general public, journalists, our children, and our family pets), I want us to consider one of the rungs on the ladder that got us all here: our negotiating skills. As with the subject of "closing argument," I have avoided writing to you on this topic for almost twelve years.

Why the delay? Because it is a tough topic. First, you all already think you know how to do it best . . . your way. Second, it's about as easy to make this subject funny as to get you chuckling at a riff of heart disease jokes. Even so, here goes.

Children do it naturally, which suggests negotiating is in our DNA . . . built into our biological hard drives. Stories here are endless. Like Tommy who proudly showed his mother the turtle he received in trade from Billy in exchange for Tommy's bicycle (Billy later became a successful plaintiff's lawyer, Tommy a mortgage derivatives trader).

They do it in every culture: negotiating for a rug in Istanbul, trinkets in Cairo, Euros in London, or explosives in Pakistan. (The last example reminds me that some negotiating relates to illegal activities. Years ago a partner of mine was the victim of an extortion attempt. The crook called him and threatened to kill his wife if he did not come up with $100,000. My partner negotiated him down to a much more sensible $20,000, and, with the help of the FBI, made the drop that caught the crook, who now lives in prison. True story. Of course, when it was all over, we chided our partner, since he might have gotten the crook down to $17,500 or maybe even $17,250. Had he lived up to his reputation for pinching every penny, he should have negotiated down the payoff and the threat. Maybe get the guy down to threatening to give her a paper cut if not paid $20 and a Subway tuna salad. A little more effort and maybe the crook would have been guilty of only a misdemeanor? Missed opportunity.)

But I digress, and the example of my partner brings me to a point. Natural or not, negotiation is a skill, and some are better at it than others. Importantly, being a skill and not just a talent, it can be taught. Yet, though it is fundamental to all we do as lawyers, we don't routinely see it taught in law school. I think it would have been nice, and my life would have been made easier, if I had been taught some negotiating rules. Regardless, I will now extend to you the favor that was denied me.

Let's focus on one type of negotiation: attempting to settle a lawsuit. Regardless of your level of skill and the tricks of the trade that work for you, here are a few basic rules:

First rule: Never lie in negotiations. Your credibility is everything, and if you get caught lying, you are lost. Now, that doesn't mean you should "show your hole cards," because the second rule is to "never disclose your hole cards." It does mean, however, to choose your words wisely. For example, if opposing counsel is so rude that he asks you if your last offer is all of your settlement authority, answer honestly that it is "every penny I am in a position to offer."

Second rule: Never disclose your hole cards. This means the other side must always be kept guessing, not only about your ultimate settlement authority, but also about what you know of the case, and his client(s). Not disclosing what you don't know always strengthens your hand. Almost every case has a secret or two that one side does not want disclosed to the other. If you act like you know "something," the other side will worry that you do know it . . . even though you don't. So keep your ignorance to yourself.

Third rule (a corollary to the second rule): At the beginning of negotiations, never offer your "top dollar" or demand your "bottom dollar," no matter how sincerely the other side asks for it "to save time, and cut to the chase." Whatever figure you present, they won't believe it is not negotiable, and you will end up taking up the whole day convincing them it really is your "top" or "bottom." Trust me, I foolishly did it once. It was the morning of the third day of trial. The second day had gone very well for us. Our opponents asked for our "non-negotiable bottom line to settle." We gave it to them. Eight hours later (yep, it took eight hours to convince them), we settled for that figure. So don't do it. No matter how tempting. Besides, no one knows what "cut to the chase" literally means anyway. Maybe it means what happened to me.

Fourth rule (a corollary to the third rule): Be patient. Every negotiation has a necessary gestation period that cannot be rushed. If you rush, you risk paying too much or getting too little. Being short, fat, and slow, I don't know much about tennis. But as an observer, I think it seems that the players that do best work from back at the baseline with long shots between them before anyone rushes up to the net, and even then they usually rush it only when the other player is in some way out of position. Same thing for negotiating. Stay back at the baseline a while, lobbing offers and receiving demands, until you get the feel for the rally and know what is going on. Remember, you are not going to settle if you do not want to, and if you do desire settlement, you are not going to pay more, or accept less, than you ultimately choose. So allowing time to let the settlement develop costs you nothing.

Fifth rule: Never look back on a deal. With any settlement you will wonder if you could have paid less or gotten more. Don't do that. You didn't pay less or get more, so such thoughts are a waste of time, and unhealthy. To avoid this natural tendency to second-guess yourself, you might use a bit of sarcasm. If asked how the settlement discussions went, say: "It was easy. I just started stuffing great wads of cash down the plaintiff's parched little throat until he cried out 'No mas!' Yep, I beat him with Benjamins." Setting aside the fact that "stuffing great wads of cash" is a remarkably effective way to successfully settle a lawsuit, when used as sarcasm and not as a negotiating strategy, saying it will help you get past second-guessing a result.

Let's stop here. There is much more to the subject. I'm sure there are whole books written on it. I've never read one, though. Their price is not negotiable.

BY LOU SCOFIELD

Tips:
Jury Selection

Summer 2008

The problem with writing the definitive article on jury selection is that, as with closing argument, every one of you thinks you know how to do it better than anyone else. Once you get to this level of big-shot courtroom lawyer you are likely, and justifiably, set in your ways. After all, jury selection is an art, not a science, with each of us using colors and brush-strokes, bold and light, that we believe work best. Still, there are a few universal rules that you forget at your peril. Some of them are:

One: Remember the rule of "P." Strike all preachers, politicians, pipefitters, and welders. I know "welders" doesn't start with a "P" but strike them anyway.

Two: Remember Luke and "trust the force." Always trust your instincts. Some call it "vibes." Some call it "intuition." Whatever you call it, no matter

how good, charming, or wonderful a prospective juror seems to be, never let on the jury someone who
gives you the creeps. In his bestselling book *Blink*,
Malcolm Gladwell will teach you to trust your gut
feelings. In it he discusses countless studies that prove
your intuitive reactions, born of experience, are well
founded and best followed.

Three: No place for pride. The jury-selection
process has so many dynamics that you can use all the
help you can get. I always recruit my client and any
other assisting folks to help with peremptory strikes.
It is remarkable what another set of eyes and ears can
pick up. In other words, sometimes your well-crafted
questions are no match for the observations made
by your client during voir dire (pronounced "vore
dye-er" not "vwa-deer" like you latté-sipping grano-
la-crunchers like to say it).

Four: Ignore the popular tricks. For example,
ignore "body language" and bumper stickers. Most
body language is useless in jury selection. No one,
including the person supposedly speaking with their
body movements, knows the "language" and it is
inherently ambiguous. Of course, if a prospective
juror is obviously mouthing to you that "you suck,"
you might consider exploring the issue further . . .
but only if you don't mind the rest of the courtroom
learning what you suck at. Risky, though, because
you don't know if the juror intends the expression
as an adjective or a verb.

More to the point, if I see a man with crossed
arms, it could mean that he has a closed mind. But

it could just as easily mean that the folks on either side of him are occupying the arm rests, or, better yet, that he likes to cross his arms. Most body language is much too subtle for me.

Then there are juror bumper stickers. Asking what is on a juror's bumper sticker only leads to more questions, such as, "Is it your car, or your son's?" "Was the sticker on there when you bought the car?" "Are you proud of it, or is it like your tattoo, something you deeply regret putting there?"

Folks, if you can't think of a better reason to strike a juror than folded arms, or if you can't think of a better question than the bumper-sticker question, you need to re-think your approach.

Five: Don't forget to use the "tried and trues." These are countless. Here's a couple: Begin your voir dire by asking each of the jurors whether they have made up their mind. Second, as time is allowed, tell the panel as much as you can about your case. (In Texas voir dire is closing argument, and if you haven't won the case by the time you sit down you are in big trouble.) Ask each juror if they can be fair, and watch each as they answer. This isn't a wasted question if you use it well. You already know your personal "tried and trues." Don't abandon them in favor of some new methodology . . . which leads us to jury consultants.

Six: Jury consultants. I have to confess to a bit of prejudice here. I think jury consultants are useful, but not for their advertised purposes. Jury consultants are an extra set of eyes and ears, which are noted above as quite useful. Beyond this they sometimes add a layer of E&O coverage, plus they might even give you a little more credibility in the eyes of an unfamiliar client.

But I have always been suspicious of the substantive benefit of jury consultants, focus groups, mock juries, summary trials, and shadow juries, because they tell you little that you didn't already know; to wit: regardless of your forum, judge, jury, facts, dazzling talents, and the ability to tell the future, any given jury can rule any way at any time. All of us have won cases that we should have lost and lost cases that we should have won. The best our experience allows us to do is suggest percentage chances of outcomes: were you to imagine the case being tried, say, ten times before ten different juries, you might say you'd expect to prevail six or seven times out of ten.

In this regard, let me tell you the Johns Manville story. Pay attention, because the way I tell it, it's almost true. The story goes that years ago Justice Parker (Fifth Circuit, retired) when he was a U.S. District Judge here in East Texas, decided to prove to the asbestos defendants, especially Johns Manville, that they could not win an asbestos case on liability. To accomplish this, five cases were brought to trial simultaneously with five juries being selected. The issues at trial were liability alone, tried simultaneously in one courtroom, before all five juries. They heard the same evidence, from the same lawyers, the same judge, the same charge, and the results were five different verdicts, ranging from the defendants being completely exonerated by one jury to a verdict finding some defendants guilty of gross negligence and exposed to punitive damages. The other juries filled in the spectrum between these two extremes. As you might imagine, I consider this little "experiment" as pretty stout justification for my suspicion of jury consultants, focus groups, mock juries, and shadow juries.

But my suspicion only goes so far. I am pro jury trial. If you exercise your strikes wisely, you will sharpen the group to some extent, and increase the likelihood that you can elevate them to their oath. It is then my personal experience that ninety percent of the time, juries do the right thing. Although half of the time they do the right thing they do it for the wrong reasons. Still and all, warts and all, a jury, more focused by your crafty jury-selection skills, will be more likely to listen favorably to your tale than a panel of arbitrators, a panel of judges, or a panel of welders.

Tips:
Questions

Summer 2005

No deep thoughts this time, fans: just a "cotton candy" piece on questions.

Courtroom lawyers are in the business of dealing in questions. Questions are the tools that we use to weave the fabric of our case. Some questions give rise to the methods we choose to use: Do I need to prove a particular fact? Is the fact relevant to the outcome of the case? How does the law allow me to prove a particular fact? Will this particular judge be sympathetic to my argument? Will the jury be offended by a particular line of questioning? What type of juror do I need?

Of course, there are peripheral questions that surround the trial of a case as well: Will my wife really leave me if I spend four weeks in trial? Will my client fire me if I win or lose? Will I be able to get to the courthouse without stopping for gas? Will the

Astros ever again win three games in a row? Such peripheral questions might cross the mind on the way to jury selection, but they are not our craft. The art of choosing our questions, choosing our words carefully, with intention, and choosing when to ask the question, is our craft.

Of course, knowing what not to ask involves skill as well. That skill could be the subject of its own article.

The purpose of this short article is merely to raise your consciousness by reminding you that questions, the tools that we use, are treacherous things that must be carefully considered before asked. Unlike media reporters, we lawyers cannot afford to be sloppy, lest we be startled by the answer we receive. For example, most of us have heard the tale of the eyewitness being cross-examined about his ability to see without his glasses. When asked:

"Mr. Smith, how far can you see without your glasses?"

Mr. Smith replied: "Well, I can see the moon. How far is that?"

A less apocryphal example comes from a case that I tried in one of the rural counties north of Beaumont. The trial involved injuries sustained in a fight at the local VFW hall. For those of you that are not familiar with such establishments in this neck of the woods, they are commonly drinking establishments. Fights, though rare, are known to take place, and most folks simply get over them. Sometimes, however, they result in litigation against the VFW Post for serving the booze, as well as the assailant for serving up the punches. In this particular trial, I began my cross-examination of an eyewitness with a question designed to develop the reason for his being at the hall, and to imply that the place was not particularly dangerous. I asked:

"Mr. Smith, when did you arrive at the hall?

Smith: "About eight p.m."

"And were you with a date?"

"No, I was with my wife."

Sloppy question, surprise answer. Of course, sloppy questions don't just occur in the courtroom. A while back one of the ladies in the office asked my daughter, Emma, how old she was:

"Five years old."

"And are you in school?"

Long pause. "Well, I was this morning, but I'm here now."

Sloppy question, surprise answer.

What these examples tell us is that questions are treacherous, and we need to be careful out there when we are asking them. Not only must we constantly re-mind ourselves to be ready for the unexpected reply to what we think is an otherwise proper question (so we do not look completely stupefied when we get the unexpected reply), but we also need to constantly remind ourselves that simply because the question can be asked does not mean that it makes any sense. Take this question for example: Stand in front of the mirror and move your right hand; the image moves its left hand. If the mirror reverses right to left, why doesn't it reverse top to bottom? (Hint: a mirror does not reverse anything, it merely reflects.)

Please also be reminded of the cautions of the great Irving Younger: "Never, ever, ask anything but leading questions," and "Never, no matter how curious you are, ask the question 'Why?'" You will certainly get an answer you are not looking for. For example, don't ask your wife why she spikes your evening drink with Focus Factor instead of Viagra. You don't really want to know the answer.

The same goes for the old theological question "Why do bad things happen to good people?"

Do you really want to know the answer? It's not "Because they do."

The answer is: "None of your business."

Fortunately for us, "none of your business" is not often an acceptable answer from a witness in the courtroom. If it were, trials would be a lot shorter.

Tips:
Speaking at a Conference

Winter 2007

Because of our lofty positions as big-shot trial lawyers, we are often called upon to speak at conferences, law schools, and various "continuing education" events. Unfortunately, many of you are not nearly as good at this as you think you are. The reason has nothing to do with intellect, courtroom skills, or physical appearance. It has to do with a bad upbringing . . . aka lack of training.

Of course, I would not presume to lecture those of you whose conference-speaking skills are legendary, but for those of you who stink at it, it might do you some good to read on. What follows is essentially a primer on the fundamentals of a good conference talk.

In general, you should first identify your audience. Trust me, the Beaumont Garden Club Men's Auxiliary will not be receptive to the same subject matter and style as the Texas Association of Defense

Counsel, regardless of what you think of Texas law-yers. The education and bias of the audience will dictate many of the elements of your talk.

Having identified the audience, you should next pick a topic. You may have had the experience of someone (usually a busybody "conference chair-man") suggesting a topic. Don't agree to it. For one thing, you'll have to learn all the law about the topic, and, if it is new to you, learning it will be harder than you think. Instead, insist on a topic you feel comfortable with, preferably one you have already spoken on at least a couple of times in the past. This way you don't have to learn as much, and you can claim you're developing an expertise on that narrow corner of the law. You'll be spoken of at cocktail par-ties: "Did you hear Scofield's talk on Property Rights to Ten-Inch Color-Variegated Coal Seams? No one knows his stuff like Scofield!"

Yes, insist on your own topic, and do it with a pompous air by suggesting to the "chairman" how well received your talk was at the Forbes Corporate President's Society. Don't feel guilty about this slight prevarication. After all, you're not getting paid.

Now that you have sized up your audience and grabbed a topic you know something about, let's get down to the details of the talk. Start by thanking your host and audience. The audience knows you don't care, but it's the starting point they expect, and with bad coffee and gummy eggs in their gut, they aren't interested in this rule being changed. And by the way, when expressing your gratitude, don't tell some stupid story about what you and the chairman did at dinner the night before. Unless it involved you getting arrested and being given a sponge bath by the Neanderthal who shared your cell, the audience doesn't care about you or the egotistical "conference chairman," much less your dinner.

Next, tell a joke . . . a joke appropriate to the audience (see above). For instance, at your next talk in Dubai, don't tell a joke about Islam, even if it's very funny. And even though by reputation folks in Dubai are slow to anger, there is nothing more embarrassing than having your best talk on the rule against perpetuities interrupted by gunfire. You're better off using a different joke.

Don't tell any joke about your spouse, your law firm, or your dog. Word will get back to them.

Old quips, sayings, and one-liners will do just fine. Here are a few I've recently stolen that you are free to use:

Why don't blind people like to skydive? Because it scares the dog. —Anonymous

Never eat more than you can lift. —Miss Piggy

Sometimes when reading Goethe I have a paralyzing suspicion that he is trying to be funny. —Davenport. Too cerebral? Try this one:

If it weren't for pickpockets I'd have no sex life at all. —Rodney Dangerfield

Having started with your joke, don't stand there looking pleased with yourself; move right in to the body of your talk. Begin with "signposting." Signposting is the act of telling your audience, in advance, what outline your talk will follow. In this way they will know when the end approaches and can program themselves for when to awaken and politely applaud. As you progress into the meat of your talk, be sure to sprinkle in examples. I love examples. We all love examples. They are like the captioned pictures in your high-school history book; they require less effort than the text. However, avoid examples that are not politically correct. Don't use as an example the disabled, Republicans, Democrats, or any person of any gender, sexual preference, or race, unless, of course, it is yourself and you're being self-deprecating.

Don't forget the "Rule of Five." This rule says that, regardless of the subject, the audience won't work with you beyond five major points. You know this rule from your jury trials. It applies to your conference talks too.

If your talk is in the form of a "panel discussion," I recommend you don't participate. Just sit there quietly. If you must participate, always talk last, and simply add to what has already been said by agreeing with the panel member who got the most applause. Just say: "I agree with Frank's point, but for different reasons." And leave it at that. Don't give any reasons. Everyone will think you are really smart . . . especially Frank.

Finally, it's time to conclude. Regardless of how much time is left, regardless of how smart you think you are, never, ever, open the floor to questions. If you do there will always be some jerk who was listening carefully, now asking you, in front of everybody, how you can possibly justify some conclusion you reached. You're the speaker; you owe no explanations. Perhaps you will finish with another joke or quip. Then get very sincere. Let the audience know how much you enjoyed yourself, and earnestly thank them for their kind attention. Remember, through it all, honesty and integrity are your most important allies. Once you learn to fake those, you'll succeed at anything (apologies to George Burns).

BY LOU SCOFIELD

Tips:
Closing Argument

Winter 2012

Tips for closing argument: For all the years I have authored this column I have avoided writing a definitive piece on closing argument because it is a treacherous topic. After all, closing argument is the "cherry" on top of the trial. It is the one point in a trial when you think you can bring your personal charisma, style, charm, intellect, knowledge, skill, and talent into play, all at the same time, all to save your client's unappreciative and underserving neck. Elsewhere in the case you can use one or more of your assets on the above list, but not all at once. Of course, if you think this, you are wrong. It is not that big a deal.

The bloated reputation of closing argument stems from two things: one, its place in the case as the last hurrah to the jury, and, two, the long, relatively uninterrupted block of time you get to stand in front of the jury and bloviate. Fact is, if you have not won your case before closing argument, you are in big trouble.

Still, it is a fun part of the case, and our delusion as to its importance makes it special . . . especially if you have a larger audience than just the jury in the courtroom. So it is worth writing about. Here goes:

Just because many of you are smarter, more successful, and/or more talented than I am, you think your way of doing it is best. It may not be, especially if in undergraduate school you were a literature or poly sci or art major. References to Shakespeare, politics, or Vermeer do not a powerful closing make.

The best closing arguments are made by folks with undergraduate degrees in geology, because the best closing arguments are nothing more than a limited string of vivid statements of the obvious. How can I say such a thing? Isn't there an expression "Only fools state the obvious"? Well, yes, but I always thought this expression to be simultaneously self-proving and insulting to its author. What's more, it is not true. Stating the obvious, very vividly, at the conclusion of the case, is our stock in trade. Amen? You have just spent a whole trial, with all its parts, developing and repeating throughout, your theory of the case and the evidence to support it. In the closing argument you remind the jury of your theory of the case, and systematically point to the evidence that proves it. You figuratively say to them: "See, I told you so. It is right here!" (while pointing up or down, whichever is appropriate).

Of course, there are some rules on how best to

do this, most of which I have stolen. Some follow:

- Start by reminding the jurors of their oath.

- Elevate them to the moment and show them your respect for them, and their role. They love this part, but only if you show them that you really mean it.

- Remind yourself that it is not all about you.

- Be yourself; don't try to be someone else. If you don't your words will ring hollow.

- Adhere to strictest honesty; never say anything not supported by the evidence. If you don't, even if you stray only once, your words will ring hollow.

- Concede what you must concede, but always follow a concession with a "But what really matters is . . ."

- Never attack opposing counsel; it makes you look weak and detracts from your case. Always do the opposite. Appreciate his or her skills. Speak of how good, and crafty, your opposition is: "Isn't Tom just the best? He could talk a cat into a swimming pool."

- Never call a witness a liar. Leave it to your jurors to do that in their deliberations. You can, however, come close by using deflective phrases. For example, you can make almost any insult palatable by adding the phrase "God bless him." Such as "Plaintiff's expert desperately kept claiming my sparks machine was defective, but God bless him, he just couldn't stick with the facts to do it." "God bless him" can be used repeatedly. It is much better than the deflective phrase "With all due respect." That phrase wears out too fast.

• Remind the jurors of what you said you would show them, and remind them where you did so.

• Cover every issue in the case. Jurors notice if you miss one and might think it a concession.

• Never have more than five main points per issue. Better to have only three. Best to have only one. No matter how many more "great points" you think you have (you will be tempted by them to violate this rule), your audience will only put up with five, tops. And won't forgive you for the rest that you drag them through.

• Respect the juror's intellect. Or to put it a bit differently, don't talk down to them. They will "get it" if you deliver the information accurately, even with complex facts.

• End with gratitude and a reminder to them of their role.

It's been said that the whole idea of closing argument is to give your jurors hooks on which to hang their arguments on your behalf in the jury room. I agree. That is why making your closing argument "a limited string of vivid statements of the obvious" works.

Finally, if you are the defense counsel in the case, in the end you will have to sit down and shut up while your opposition gets to close. Two things to deal with this sorry fact: First, say this when you close: "Now I'm out of time. Because the plaintiff has the burden of proof, they have the last turn at speaking to you. Like a mule in a hailstorm I just have to take it, without a chance to counter whatever he says. So as he's talking, I ask each of you to remember the evidence, and that I would have plenty to say about it if I had another turn." Second, always interrupt the plaintiff's final closing, even if just to show your flag. It is not improper because, without fail, plaintiff's counsel will always say something in the final closing that will invite, or even require, a speaking objection. Ahem.

Tips: *Pro Hac Vice,* Stranger in a Strange Land

Winter 2008

Now that we are all big-shot courtroom lawyers, it was only a matter of time before our talents would be discovered by our clients. Among them are "special clients" who recognize our talents even more (as though such were possible) than the rest of our clients. I am referring to those special clients who call upon us to travel to jurisdictions far from our home and comfortable puddle to try cases in "foreign" courts. By "foreign" I mean any courtroom situated more than one hundred fifty miles from your personal legal epicenter.

Some clients ask us to do this because they like us. They like us because we've been successful for them in the past, we know the product or issues involved, and they don't want to pay to educate another English major about a particular profession, or physics, or engineering, or chemistry. They like us because we're cheap (er—not me, of course) or because we have their trust. But most of all I prefer to think they like us because we are oozing with more talent than anyone else they could call on for the task.

Regardless of the reason, many of you are called upon by your clients to handle cases in distant places. Some of you have not yet had this happen, but you will. The purpose of this article is to offer, for the benefit of the practiced and the neophyte, some observations on practicing elsewhere from where one is.

I have some credentials in this regard. I am national counsel for one client and regional counsel for a number of others. As a regional counsel I go places in Texas far from MehaffyWeber's flagship office in Beaumont. Lest some of you think regional counsel is a lesser distinction, it isn't in Texas. I am regional Texas counsel for a motor-vehicle manufacturer for an area ranging from San Antonio and Austin east to Beaumont and the river between Texas and Louisiana, north to Dallas, and south to Brownsville and South Padre Island. That's an area the size of Vermont, New Hampshire, Massachusetts, Connecticut, Rhode Island, eastern New York State, and all of the habitable portions of Alaska combined. Perhaps a slight exaggeration, but you get the point, and I can promise you there are places I go in Texas that are every bit as foreign to me as is Boise, Idaho. And whether regional or national in range, they all share the same demands.

Demand One: Get a local counsel. Even if you are licensed in the jurisdiction, if you are one hundred fifty miles from home you are going to get your keister (euphemism for "ass") handed to you if you don't have local counsel. I'm reminded of the case where a Dallas lawyer came down to Beaumont, tried his case, and in closing argument said to a jury on which he had left pipefitters, welders, and ironworkers . . . I kid you not . . . : "I want you to try to resist me. Yes, resist me . . . " They did. The biases, strengths, and weaknesses of the local jurors and the judge, and the foibles and proclivities of the other counsel, are all vital information. What sells and what doesn't is vital information that you need and don't have. If you don't already have an attorney friend to fill the role of local counsel, try to hire the judge's daughter or son-in-law. Not to influence the court unfairly; of course not, that would be unethical. Perhaps just to assist in leveling the playing field. No luck? Then try to find someone smarter than you. Don't worry, there are lots of them. He or she will be a big help in all stages of the case and you won't feel as bad when you start to drive off at its conclusion and you overhear muttering: "National counsel, huh? That idiot had nothing over me."

Demand Two: Learn the local rules and the local substantive law. Few things are more embarrassing than learning for the first time at the charge conference that Oklahoma doesn't have comparative fault as a defense in a product liability claim. Or that a local court in Kentucky doesn't hear motions in limine until after voir dire. If an admission *pro hac vice* is needed you'll have to learn the local law and rules anyway, because in virtually all cases you promise the admitting court that you have at least read them. And you don't want to break that promise. And on the topic of *pro hac vice*, your local counsel is really handy here, because in some places he'll actually have to swear you are of good moral character. Some of you can't even get your spouses to say that about you.

Demand Three: Use your foreign status to your advantage. You can extract sympathy and gain accommodations from the other lawyers in the case. After all, you have to travel far and at great inconvenience to do anything. Human nature will incline most lawyers to avoid cancellations and flex to your schedule in a way they would not for just local folks for whom familiarity has bred contempt. You're the new kid, and, strangely enough, they will simultaneously presume innocence on your part while also thinking you must be some big gun. This is a huge advantage. I had a case in New York. I promise you, the local Bar there had never seen anything like me. You know, Texas drawl, quick smile, fumbling at my notes in the plaintiff's deposition. By the time the plaintiff's counsel was on his feet shouting objections, the damage had been done. Naturally my line of questions was proper in Texas, but apparently a big "no-no" in New York, even though not technically a violation of local rules. But hey, I'm the new kid. And here again local counsel comes in really handy. He took a recess, and we left the room and opposing counsel behind, trying to control his blood pressure. My local counsel explained the different culture, cleared it up with opposing counsel by pointing out my innocence and ignorance of local custom, and we resumed. Great, eh? Being foreign has its plusses.

Demand Four, the final demand for purposes of this column: Never forget where you are. You may start to feel at home. Your local counsel, the court, and the other lawyers may work hard to make you feel that way. But you are not at home, and while your reputation may be magnified, so will your mistakes. It's like walking around on Mars and thinking, "Gee, this is just like the Mojave." Don't flip up your visor to see better. You are not on Earth; you are not local. When in foreign courts be relentless in asking your local counsel about any and every step you take. Local procedures, the substance of your case, how he thinks the court, jurors, or lawyers will react to your ideas or strategies. Ask about everything. It will repeatedly confirm to all that you are not local, but, trust me, the locals in the case will never see you as "local" anyway.

I hope these little tips are of some help. My travels have confirmed for me that in a general sense we are all the same, but simultaneously every local legal culture is different. They each have their own long history, customs, and unwritten rules. Frankly, I think this is a great thing. It lets the practice of law flex to the environment it is in. And you'll do well for your clients in these differing environments if you allow yourself to be flexible too. The best fun, though, is the people you meet. As all us traveling salesmen know, every one is a blessing.

BY LOU SCOFIELD

Better People Than We Think

Summer 2003

First a little housekeeping: I enjoy receiving the letters and e-mails regarding past writings in this column, especially those that are flattering. If you are inspired to write something critical, such as correspondence that uses certain verbs as nouns, please direct them to the attention of the publisher and not the undersigned.

Now, dear readers, our topic for the day is a simple proposition: as a people, we are better than we think we are. This shocking revelation derives from a recent survey reported on the radio, and heard by me as I drove the long trek home from Houston to the small hamlet of Beaumont, Texas. For the uninitiated among you, the radio is where all competent lawyers learn half of their knowledge of the law, most of their knowledge of medicine, and all of their knowledge of philosophy. If, on the road, you are wasting your valuable time listening to music or books on tape, you will be viewed as strangely backward and ignorant of the truly important features of the world.

On the day in question, the radio newsman announced: "A survey showed eighty percent of Americans believe in angels."

Despite the explosive impact of this piece of information, I managed to keep the car on the road. Imagine that—eighty percent of us believe in angels. How could that be? I'm sure some of the survey respondents did not understand the question and thought it referred to the California baseball team.

Even so, eighty percent is a startlingly high percentage, and it speaks volumes to how we are doing as a people. In order for eighty percent of us to believe in angels, there must be a lot of us who have experienced them: either in the form of other people who came through under dark and desperate circumstances; or in the form seen in children and grandchildren, and noticed in the flicker of heavenly mischief in their eyes; or perhaps others have witnessed the whole shebang . . . radiant light, feathers, booming voices, etc. And still there must be others who have not witnessed an angel themselves but are imbued with a remarkable hope or faith that allows them to express a belief in angels. Think about it a minute. If there is any truth at all to the statistic, even if the statistic is off "plus or minus ten percent," such a huge majority of us have witnessed truly good behavior on the part of others that it allows expression of a belief in angels.

Of course, a poll result does not prove that an-

gels exist. The cynical among you will view the statistic as confirmation of the persistent stupidity and
irrationality of humans. For the twenty percent in the
survey who responded that they did not believe in
angels, or did not know, this must be an awfully dark
world to muddle around in. No wonder they listen to
books on tape.

I, for one, am part of the eighty percent, not
because I "believe" or "have faith" in angels. Rather
because I have seen and spoken to some, though I did
not know they were angels at the time. If you have
not had such an experience, I can give you a little
assistance in "angel spotting":

Typically angels are well dressed and well spoken. Angels aren't pushy unless they are carrying a
specific message from the Boss. They seem to usually
work alone. I have never seen more than one at a
time. It is not clear to me whether they prefer being
alone or are spread so thin (what with the population
explosion and all) that they can't really pair up. Regardless of their age, I've never seen one driving, so
I suspect they are not allowed to drive. I'm sure that
cuts down on traffic violations and fines that would
need to be "fixed" by intermediate levels of angel
supervision.

Of the angels that I have seen, most were well
kempt and appeared of better-than-average intellect. No flea-bitten, bad-smelling, raggedy types
sent down just to fake us out and test us. In every
experience that I have had, the angel had simple
words. The words were either of assurance or soft-

ly spoken sound advice.

Most that I have seen do look a bit pale. I don't recall ever seeing one on the beach or coming out of Florida Tans wearing sunglasses and drinking a Diet Coke. In fact, most have been wearing coats, no doubt to hide attachments. (For those of you who haven't seen the movie Michael, you are in for a treat. Still, the angels that I have seen look nothing like John Travolta.) And your final "angel spotting" tip: If you think you see one, check out the shoes. All angels wear comfortable shoes.

So eighty percent of us believe in angels. Remarkable. Even if you've never seen one, even if there aren't any, doesn't it speak well for what we are seeing in one another? Maybe, as a people, we are better than we think we are.

Now I have to drop this reverie and go take a plaintiff's deposition in a case where she faked the accident. I'll bet her shoes hurt her feet.

BY LOU SCOFIELD

Getting Older

Fall 2015

I attended a school-sponsored seminar with my daughter. It was on the subject of human trafficking. It being a light news day, a local television station attended and filmed excerpts for the evening news, complete with audience shots. The next day I had countless visitors telling me that they saw me on the news. Some had it on their smartphones, and showed me. The shot was zoomed in on me, and had below it the feature title: "Human Traffickers." The graphics were done in such a way that a casual observer could only interpret what they were seeing as an example of a real live "Human Trafficker"! They might just as well have said: "Yep, this is what one looks like. So, Mothers, when you see this man in your neighborhood, hustle the kids into the house and call the cops."

So much for a lifetime as a pillar of the community. So much for building and guarding my reputation for decency and honor.

But that is not what really bothered me about the episode. What bothered me was that I did not want to recognize that short, chubby old man depicted in the shot as being me. I did . . . but I didn't. Part of me wanted to say, "Who the heck is that geezer?" But (sigh) I knew. Then in rushed the next thoughts: "What happened? What happened to that thin, smart, longer-haired blond guy with a quick wit and a wild and dangerous look in his eye?" "I'm still here," said a small voice inside, "but stuffed into the body of a geezer guy who looks like a Human Trafficker."

In light of the foregoing episode, I decided to make this column a very short one that relates to growing old in the law practice. And despite some obvious "downsides" of aging (see above), I have decided to limit myself to the "upsides" of growing old in the law practice.

One positive is the deference others now give me. No, I'm not talking about the "senior coffee" at the Whataburger stand . . . although that is nice. I'm talking about deference by the courts. For example, when I was starting out and had a hearing on some subject, I'd complete my argument to the judge and he'd inquire, "Well, Lou, do you have any cases or other authorities for that?" Today, under the same circumstances, I'll complete my argument and a typical judge will say, "Well?" and look over the top of his glasses at my opponent for a response.

It's not just deference from judges. I get it from

some other lawyers, too. I am frequently involved in multi-party cases and I've noticed that in depositions my limitations from being a geezer are often useful. Like getting the plaintiff to repeat a harmful admission because "I didn't hear his answer." Or getting my client to stop and think during a damaging stretch of interrogation by opposing counsel by imposing on opposing counsel to repeat his question. After all, I didn't hear it.

No one would have bought it when I was thirty. But now . . .

And then there is the advantage of disability. Now that I dodder around with a cane, I look more disabled than most plaintiffs, and my impairments can't help but influence a jury considering damages. After all, by comparison, many plaintiffs look "fit as a fiddle."

And then there is the money. It is a strange phenomenon that when I was young, strong, and sharp as a tack, I was worth less per hour than I am now. By virtue of years of inspired victories and years of brutal defeats, some sort of fairy dust got sprinkled upon me that gives me great value. Like on the PBS Antiques Roadshow where the beat-up old furniture that has never been re-finished is somehow priceless, I have become something that, by virtue of the old patina or tarnish, is worth more than something new . . . not that I'd draw much at an auction . . . but you get my point. And I must tell you that getting paid in part for what you know, and not just for what you do, is very nice.

So all in all, the process of growing old in the law

practice is not so bad, and is less bad than the option of not growing old in the law practice.

Ordinarily I would have ended this column with the corny joke in the last sentence above. But I re-read this piece and realized that, while those of you who know me may get a chuckle out of the "Human Trafficker" story, I have not yet actually met most of you. So it may be necessary for me say . . . this is very embarrassing to have to do this . . . no, I am not a human trafficker. How do you know? After all, it was on the news. You know because I am a member of this organization. You can't get into this club if you have more than a couple of recent felonies.

Final Advice

Summer 2017

"Impostor syndrome" is a condition suffered by some very competent, high-achieving individuals who are marked by an inability to internalize their skills and accomplishments, and suffer from a persistent irrational fear of being exposed as a "fraud" (definition mostly stolen from Wikipedia, 2017). As members of one of the most critical professions in the country, all of you are high achievers . . . so many of you may have suffered from this syndrome for a moment or two in your careers.

I, fortunately, do not suffer from this malady, owing to three things.

One: As a law student, when I had some time to kill, I would occasionally ease on down to the courthouse and watch some trials. It took little time to realize that even I (a mere student) could do a better job than some of the talent I observed there.

Two: I adhere to the lesson in the tale of the two hikers who came upon an angry grizzly bear preparing to charge. As one quickly shed his boots and donned his tennis shoes, the other said, "You can't outrun that bear." "You're right," replied the first, "but I only have to outrun you." The point being, we don't have to be perfect, just better than our opponent.

Three: I saw a psychiatrist/author on CSPAN (I learn all of my psychiatry on CSPAN; don't you?) who spoke of a study that showed that people most sure of their own opinions are often the most ignorant, and since they also do not engage in reflective thinking, they are less apt to question their own thoughts or abilities. It is a gift with which we ignorant, shallow thinkers are blessed, and which graces me with the ability to avoid lots of "syndromes" suffered by you high achievers.

It is from this perspective that I can have the unmitigated gall to think that I, twice a year in this column, have something useful to say to you, my dear readership. So here we go again—this time, some random (truly unrelated) tidbits of advice on life and sometimes law. (Be advised, I have stolen every one of these.)

• Always treat everyone with decency and respect: lawyers, judges, jurors, parties, clerks, clients, and witnesses (except for an "expert" witness who is testifying falsely for money; such are fair game). God expects us to treat each other well.

• Never run for political office; you might win.

• If you wonder if it's ethical, don't do it.

- Don't ever start believing your own B.S.
- Never do anything solely for the money.
- At the very beginning of every case, identify and write out the jury questions (issues) under the law governing your case, long before you start advising your client or slinging discovery at the other side.
- Never press deadlines; complete everything a week before it is due.
- Repeat yourself. Repeat yourself.
- Ask only leading questions . . . ever, especially at cocktail parties.
- Plaintiffs never "suffer" an injury; they only "sustain" them (unless it is your injury, or you represent the injured plaintiff).
- Always try to come up with something new to use in every case.
- If called by a panther, don't anther. —Ogden Nash
- Have a hard-copy backup ready for failed courtroom technology. (Example: poster boards of PowerPoints at the ready in case the "system" crashes—and it will. Plus, have a tech person handy for the jury to hate instead of you when the system crashes—and it will.)
- If you want to stay happy, do not read "The Love Song of J. Alfred Prufrock" by T.S. Eliot.
- Last thing: When all else is done, and you think you are ready (for anything: trial, appellate argument, marriage proposal), take a moment and ask yourself: What is not there, what is missing? It always helps to identify what was not said or done

but should have been. When you do, there is always gold when you figure out why.

So there you have it: with the advice above, coupled with all of the information from my prior columns, you now know everything you need to know to become a sparkling lawyer who will never suffer (or suffer again) from "imposter syndrome." In view of this, and since I have written all that can be written, this is my last installment of A Word From Lou. Over these years you have dragged yourself through almost thirty columns (I lost count) on topics ranging from how to be a boss, jury selection, mugging it up to the press, war stories, closing argument, giving a seminar presentation, and The Bear Story. It has been great fun. Thank you for reading them.

ACKNOWLEDGMENTS

Since a book does not simply "happen" onto the scene, I should be ashamed of myself if I failed to express my gratitude to some of those who made this come about.

I am grateful to the first victims of these writings, the members of the Association of Defense Trial Attorneys (ADTA), who were exposed to them twice a year for 15 years in *The Association Press*, and who did not rally to purge them (such was their desperation for any reading material).

I am grateful to my law partners and friends at MehaffyWeber. For more than 40 years they have been the foundation for the professional and personal experiences yielding much of what you will find in this book.

I am grateful to my secretary, Jodie, who helped me put these columns together, and also kept track of them as they accumulated year after year.

I am grateful to Professor of Law Bridget Fuselier, Baylor Law, who took the time to review these writings and suggest rational organization of them.

I am grateful to my friend Tanner Hunt, attorney and Renaissance man, who took the time to read the first assembled manuscript and offer his wise thoughts, in his usual witty way.

I am grateful to Joseph Daniel and the talented people at Story Arts Media, who applied their remarkable knowledge and skills to refine, then produce, this book.

I am grateful to my family especially for their love (some of whom, incidentally, find themselves discussed in the preceding pages).

I am grateful to God for the gift of this life, for the gift of humor, and for grace. I wish these gifts for everyone.

L.S.